THE
BHAGAVAD GITA
THE SONG OF GOD

THE
BHAGAVAD GITA
THE SONG OF GOD

translated by
ABBOT GEORGE BURKE
(SWAMI NIRMALANANDA GIRI)

LIGHT ᴼᶠ ᴛʜᴇ SPIRIT
PRESS
CEDAR CREST, NEW MEXICO

Published by
    Light of the Spirit Press
    lightofthespiritpress.com

    Light of the Spirit Monastery
    P. O. Box 1370
    Cedar Crest, New Mexico 87008
    www.ocoy.org

ISBN-13: 978-0998599816
ISBN-10: 0998599816

Library of Congress Control Number: 2017901669
Light of the Spirit Press, Cedar Crest, New Mexico

1. REL032030 RELIGION / Hinduism / Sacred Writings
2. OCC021000 BODY, MIND & SPIRIT / Reference

First edition, (February 2017)

Credits: The cover contains a detail of a painting of Krisha and
Arjuna on the Battlefield of Kurukshetra by the Rajasthani artist
Bhanwar lal Girdhari lal Sharma

CONTENTS

Preface

Bhagavad Gita–The Book of Life

Several thousand years ago in north-central India, two people sat in a chariot in the midpoint of a great battlefield. One of them, the yogi Arjuna, knew that it would be not be long before the conflict would begin. So he asked Krishna, the Master of Yoga, what should be his attitude and perspective in this moment. And above all: What should he do?

There was no time to spare in empty words. In a brief discourse, later turned into seven hundred Sanskrit verses by the sage Vyasa, Krishna outlined to Arjuna the way to live an entire life so as to gain perfect self-knowledge and self-mastery.

The battle was ferocious and everyone lost. Only a handful remained alive. But when Vyasa wrote his epic poem, the Mahabharata, he put Krishna's inspired words into it as a precious jewel. Instantly they were extracted, named The Song of God (Bhagavad Gita), and circulated throughout the subcontinent.

That was several thousand years ago, and today the Gita is found in households throughout India and has been translated into every major language of the world. Literally billions of copies have been handwritten and printed. (A few years ago a spiritual organization in South Africa printed one million copies for free distribution!)

What is the appeal of the Gita? First of all, it is totally practical, free of any vague or abstract philosophy. During my first trip to India over fifty years ago, I heard about a yogi who lived in a small houseboat on the Ganges river in the holy city of Benares (Varanasi). He never spoke or wrote; yet every day for many years people came to him for advice. How did he manage? He had a copy of the Bhagavad Gita, and after he was told the problem or question he would open the book and point to a portion. And the inquirer would have a perfect and complete solution to the trouble.

My own spiritual awakening began by kicking me out of the nest of comfortable religion into a vast world of realities I had no idea how to cope with. I floundered around in the sea of my new horizons until one day I bought a copy of Swami Prabhavananda's translation of the Bhagavad Gita (which is still my favorite translation). I did not read it, I inhaled it. I was not reading the words of a long-dead teacher: my own Self was talking to me in the pages of that little book. Nor did I learn anything from the Gita–I remembered that which I had always known. Eternal Self spoke Eternal Truth. The Bhagavad Gita changed my life by giving me Life. Life that has never ended.

Nothing has ever arisen in my life, internal or external, that the Gita has not made clear and enabled me to deal with or understand. Yet is it not dogmatic. At the very end Krishna says to Arjuna: "Now I have taught you that wisdom which is the secret of secrets. Ponder it carefully. Then act as you think best." No threats, no promises, no coercion. It is all in the reader's hands. Even better: the Bhagavad Gita tells us that we can attain a Knowing beyond even what it tells us. And it shows us the way.

Some years ago I arranged the text of the Gita according to the meter of the original Sanskrit so it could be sung as part of the daily routine of our ashram, as is usual in many of the ashrams of India. It was also recorded, and those who heard the recording commented that they were surprised at the accuracy of the translation. So it occurred to me that if I went through and took out the meter, adding anything that had been omitted to keep the meter and making logical adjustments to clarify the meaning further, it might be of value to others. As it turned out, I made changes and adjustments to virtually every verse. And here it is. I hope you will use the glossary to assist in your understanding of what you read, because some Sanskrit words must be included in the text because they have no English equivalents, and to use words with only approximate meanings will obscure the meaning of the text.

The background of the Gita

The present text of Mahabharata takes a hundred thousand verses to give us the background and aftermath of the Great Indian War which took place at Kurukshetra in Northern India in what is the modern state of Harayana. On one side were the supporters of the Pandavas, the righteous family led by the warrior-yogi Arjuna. The opposing side were the supporters of the Kauravas, the unrighteous relatives of the Pandavas led by the heinous Duryodhana, son of the blind king Dhritarashtra.

Krishna, the king of Dwaraka in Western India (the present day state of Gujarat), was the charioteer of Arjuna. Both sides were related to each other, so whoever won the war could only do so by killing their own relatives. The Pandavas were vastly outnumbered by the Kauravas, many of whom were virtuous and respected men who were only on the Kaurava side because of previous alliances and agreements–much like the tangle which dragged good and worthy men into both sides of the First World War.

Vyasa the supreme master yogi had given the courtier Sanjaya the ability to see and hear what took place on the battlefield. When King Dritarashtra asked him to relay the events, he did so, concentrating on the dialogue of Arjuna and Krishna.

The Gita opens with Arjuna asking Krishna to drive his chariot between the armies so he can see those he must engage in war. The battlefield is still there, and so is the aura of both the terrible slaughter and the glorious revelation of Lord Krishna's immortal and eternal discourse. I recommend pilgrimage to that sacred spot which today is outwardly tranquil and pleasing to the sight. On the place where Arjuna and Krishna viewed those about to fight is a great bronze statue of Arjuna, Krishna and their chariot. (When I was there only a huge tree and a large marble replica of the chariot marked where they sat.)

But a greater pilgrimage can be made by anyone anywhere in the world by simply reading The Holy Song of God, the Srimad Bhagavad Gita. It will be a holy pilgrimage of mind and spirit. Once more the grief of Arjuna and the wisdom of Krishna will be witnessed. Those who assimilate that wisdom will come to experience for themselves the truth of the final verse of the Gita: "Wherever is Krishna, Yoga's Lord, wherever is Arjuna the bowman, there will surely (forever) be splendor, victory, wealth, and righteousness."

A practical suggestion

In the West we have the idea that spiritual texts have but one meaning, and that may be so for some, but this is not at all the case for Sanskrit texts which are intended to have multi-level messages and subtle nuances. Words which carry several relevant ideas are ideal for the profound wisdom of the Gita and Upanishads, particularly.

Because of this I recommend that you obtain translations of the Gita that contain the Sanskrit text with word-by-word translations as well as the usual verse form. Three excellent ones are those of Swami Sivananda, Swami Swarupananda and Winthrop Sargeant. In addition you need some Sanskrit dictionaries. I recommend: *A Concise Dictionary of Indian Philosophy* by John Grimes, *The Yoga-Vedanta Dictionary* of Swami Sivananda, *Sanskrit Glossary of Yogic Terms* by Swami Yogakanti and *A Sanskrit Dictionary* by John M. Denton. And my own endeavor, *A Brief Sanskrit Glossary,* is certainly helpful, and definitely complements them.

Please consult the glossary in this book about any unfamiliar Sanskrit words.

Abbot George Burke
(Swami Nirmalananda Giri)

Chapter One

THE YOGA OF THE DESPONDENCY OF ARJUNA

Dhritarashtra said:
Assembled there on dharma's field–Kurukshetra–desiring war, what did my sons and the Pandavas, O Sanjaya? (1:1)

Sanjaya said:
King Duryodhana, seeing the Pandava forces ranged ready for battle, approaching his teacher, Drona, spoke these words: (1:2)

Behold, O Teacher, this great army of Pandu's sons, assembled by Arjuna your brilliant pupil. (1:3)

Here are heroes, mighty archers, Bhima and Arjuna's equals, Yuyudhana and Virata, and Drupada the great car warrior, (1:4)

Drishtaketu, Chekitana, and the valiant King of Kashi, Purujit and Kuntibhoja, and Shaibya: the mightiest among men, (1:5)

And courageous Yudhamanyu, and valorous Uttamaujas;

the son of Shubhadra and the sons of Draupadi: all great car warriors. (1:6)

Those of ours who are indeed distinguished now know. O highest of the twice-born, the leaders of my army I now I recount unto you by name. (1:7)

Your Lordship and Bhishma and Karna and Kripa, victorious in war, Ashwattama and Vikarna, and the son of Somadatta also. (1:8)

And many other heroes, whose lives are risked for my sake, ready to discharge various weapons, all very skilled in battle. (1:9)

Sufficient is that force of ours guarded by Bhishma; insufficient, though, is that force guarded by Bhima. (1:10)

Stationed in your proper places, whatever be your positions, certainly all of you: protect Bhishma. (1:11)

To make Duryodhana happy, the aged Kuru grandsire, Bhishma, bellowing with a tremendous sound of a lion's roar, then blew his conch with great power, making a tremendous sound. (1:12)

Thereupon the Kurus' conches and kettledrums and cymbals and trumpets were sounded all at once, producing a tumultuous uproar. (1:13)

Then Krishna and Arjuna, standing in the great chariot that was yoked with the white horses, sounded forth their divine conches. (1:14)

Krishna blew Panchajanya, Arjuna blew Devadatta, and Bhima of ferocious deeds blew the great conch, Paundra. (1:15)

King Yudhishthira, Kunti's son, blew on Anantavijaya,

Nakula and Sahadeva blew on Sughosha and Manipushpaka. (1:16)

And Kashi's king, the supreme bowman, and the great warrior Shikhandi, and Dhristadyumna and Virata, and the invincible Satyaki, (1:17)

And Drupada and the sons of Draupadi, O Lord of the Earth, and Shubhadra's son, the mighty-armed, each blew upon his conch. (1:18)

Throughout the sky and the earth resounded the terrific noise which rent asunder the hearts of those in Dhritarashtra's ranks. (1:19)

Then seeing Dhritarashtra's ranks drawn up in battle array for the forthcoming clash of weapons, Arjuna took up his bow, (1:20)

And said unto Krishna: O Lord of the earth, drive my chariot to stand in the midst between the two armies, (1:21)

Until I can behold these battle-hungry men arrayed here with whom I must fight in this conflict. (1:22)

I would behold those who are about to give battle, having assembled here wishing to do service in warfare for the evil-minded son of Dhritarashtra. (1:23)

Thus addressed by Arjuna, Krishna brought the chief chariot to stand in the midst of the two armies. (1:24)

Thus facing Bhishma, Drona, and all the rulers of the earth, Krishna said: Behold, Arjuna, these Kurus assembled here. (1:25)

Arjuna saw standing there fathers, grandfathers, teachers, maternal uncles, brothers, sons, grandsons as well as friends, (1:26)

Fathers-in-law and companions in the two armies. In both of them he saw all who were relatives arrayed. (1:27)

Then filled with profound pity, desponding, he said: O Krishna, seeing my own people standing near, desiring to fight, (1:28)

My limbs sink down, my mouth dries up, my body trembles, and my hair stands on end. (1:29)

My bow drops from my hand, my skin is burning, I am unable to stand; my mind is reeling. (1:30)

Inauspicious omens I mark, and not good fortune do I foresee, if I should kill my own kinsmen in war. (1:31)

I do not desire victory, nor kingship and pleasures. What is kingship to us? What are enjoyments or even life? (1:32)

Those for whose sake we should desire kingship, enjoyments and pleasures, are arrayed in battle, abandoning their lives and riches: (1:33)

Teachers, fathers, sons, grandfathers, maternal uncles, fathers-in-law, grandsons, brothers-in-law, and other kinsmen, too. (1:34)

I do not desire to kill them who are about to kill–not even for the sovereignty of the three worlds; how then for the earth? (1:35)

What pleasure could the striking down of Dhritarashtra's sons be to us? Having killed these aggressors, evil would thus cling to us. (1:36)

Therefore we are not justified to kill the sons of Dhritarashtra, our own kinsmen. Indeed, having killed our own people, how could we be happy? (1:37)

Even if those whose thoughts are overpowered by greed do not see the wrong caused by the destruction of the family, and the crime of treachery to friends, (1:38)

Why should we not know to turn back from this evil through discernment of the evil caused by the destruction of the family? (1:39)

In the destruction of the family, the long-established family dharmas perish. When dharma perishes, adharma predominates in the entire family. (1:40)

From overpowering by adharma the women of the family are corrupted. When the women are corrupted, the intermixture of caste is born. (1:41)

Intermixture brings to hell the family destroyers and the family, too. Indeed their ancestors fall from heaven back to earthly rebirth, deprived of offerings of rice and water. (1:42)

By these wrongs of the family's destroyers, producing intermixture of caste, caste dharmas and long-established family dharmas are obliterated. (1:43)

Those whose family dharmas have been obliterated dwell indefinitely in hell–thus have we heard repeatedly. (1:44)

Ah! Alas! we are resolved to do great evil with our greed for royal pleasures, intent on killing our own people. (1:45)

If the armed sons of Dhritarashtra should kill me in battle, unresisting and unarmed, this would be a greater happiness for me. (1:46)

Thus having spoken, Arjuna, in the battle which had already begun, sat down upon the chariot seat, throwing down both arrow and bow, with a heart overcome by sorrow. (1:47)

Om Tat Sat

Thus in the Upanishads of the glorious Bhagavad Gita, the science of the Eternal, the scripture of Yoga, the dialogue between Sri Krishna and Arjuna, ends the first discourse entitled: The Yoga of the Despondency of Arjuna.

Chapter Two

SANKHYA YOGA

Sanjaya said:

To him who was thus overcome by pity, whose eyes were filled with tears, downcast and despairing, Krishna spoke these words: (2:1)

The Holy Lord said:

Whence has come this faintheartedness of yours in the time of danger–ignoble, not leading to heaven, but to disgrace? (2:2)

At no time should you entertain such cowardice–it is unsuitable in you. Abandon this base faintheartedness and stand up. (2:3)

Arjuna said:

But how can I in battle fight with arrows against Bhishma and Drona, who are worthy of reverence? (2:4)

Better that I eat the food of beggary in this world instead of my slaying these great and noble gurus. If I should kill them, desirous for gain, in truth here on earth I would enjoy pleasures stained with blood. (2:5)

We know not which is preferable: whether we should conquer them, or they should conquer us. The sons of Dhritarashtra stand facing us after slaying whom we would not wish to live. (2:6)

Weakness and pity overcome my being; with mind in confusion as to my duty, I supplicate you: Beyond doubt tell me which is preferable. I am your disciple; do you direct me. (2:7)

Truly, I see nothing that can remove this sorrow that dries up my senses, though I should attain on earth unrivalled and prosperous dominion, or even the sovereignty of the gods. (2:8)

Sanjaya said:

Thus having addressed Krishna, Arjuna said, "I shall not fight," and became totally silent. (2:9)

To him who thus was despondent in the midst of the two armies, smiling, Krishna spoke these words: (2:10)

The Holy Lord said:

You have been mourning for those who should not be mourned for, though you speak words of wisdom. The wise mourn neither the living or the dead. (2:11)

Truly there never was a time when I was not, nor you, nor these lords of men–nor in the future will there be a time when we shall cease to be. (2:12)

As to the embodied person childhood, youth and old age arise in turn, so he gets another body–the wise are not deluded by this. (2:13)

Truly, material sensations produce cold, heat, pleasure and pain. Impermanent, they come and go; you must endeavor to endure them. (2:14)

Truly, the man whom these sensations do not afflict, the same in pain and pleasure, that wise one is fit for immortality. (2:15)

It is known that the unreal never comes to be, and the real never ceases to be. The certainty of both of these principles is seen by those who see the truth. (2:16)

Know indeed that That by which all this universe is pervaded is indestructible. There is no one whatsoever capable of the destruction of the Eternal. (2:17)

These bodies inhabited by the eternal, indestructible, immeasurable, embodied Self are said to come to an end. Therefore, fight! (2:18)

He who thinks the Self is the slayer and he who thinks the Self is slain: neither of the two understands. The Self slays not, nor is it slain. (2:19)

Neither is the Self slain, nor yet does it die at any time; nor having been will it ever come not to be. Birthless, eternal, perpetual, primeval, it is not slain whenever the body is slain. (2:20)

In what way can he who knows this Self to be indestructible, eternal, birthless and imperishable, slay or cause to be slain? (2:21)

Even as a man casts off his worn-out clothes and then clothes himself in others which are new, so the embodied casts off worn-out bodies and then enters into others which are new. (2:22)

This Self by weapons is cut not; this Self by fire is burnt not;

this Self by water is wet not; and this Self is by wind dried not. (2:23)

This Self cannot be cut, burnt, wetted, nor dried. This primeval Self is eternal, all-pervading, and immovable. (2:24)

Unmanifest, unthinkable, this Self is called unchangeable. Therefore, knowing this to be such, you should not mourn. (2:25)

And moreover, if you think this Self to have constant birth and death, even then you should not mourn. (2:26)

Of the born, death is certain; of the dead, birth is certain. Therefore, over the inevitable you should not grieve. (2:27)

Beings are unmanifest in their beginning, manifest in their middle state and again unmanifest in their end. What lamentation can be made over this? (2:28)

Some perceive this Self as wondrous, another speaks of it as wondrous, another hears of it as wondrous, but even having heard of this Self, no one knows it. (2:29)

This embodied Self is eternally indestructible in the body of all. Therefore you should not mourn for any being. (2:30)

And just considering your swadharma, you should not waver, for truly to a kshatriya there is nothing greater to find than a righteous battle. (2:31)

Happy are the kshatriyas to whom heaven's gate opens when by good fortune they encounter such a battle. (2:32)

Now if you shall not undertake this dharmic engagement, then having avoided your swadharma and glory, you shall incur evil. (2:33)

And people will forever tell of your undying infamy. For the renowned, such disgrace is worse than dying. (2:34)

The great car-warriors will believe you abstain from delight in battle through fear. And among those who have thought much of you, you shall come to be lightly esteemed. (2:35)

Your enemies shall speak of you many things that should not be said, deriding your adequacy. What, indeed, could be a greater suffering than that? (2:36)

If you are slain you shall attain heaven; if you conquer you shall enjoy the earth. Therefore, stand up resolved to fight. (2:37)

Considering pleasure and pain, gain and loss, victory and defeat the same, then engage in battle. Thus you shall not incur evil. (2:38)

This buddhi yoga taught by Sankhya is now declared to you, so heed. Yoked to this buddhi yoga, you shall avoid the bonds of karma. (2:39)

In this no effort is lost, nor are adverse results produced. Even a little of this dharma protects from great fear. (2:40)

In this matter there is a single, resolute understanding. The thoughts of the irresolute are many-branched, truly endless. (2:41)

The ignorant, delighting in the word of the Veda, proclaim this flowery speech: "There is nothing else." (2:42)

Those of desire-filled natures, intent on heaven, offering rebirth as actions' fruit, performing many and various rites, are aimed at the goal of enjoyment and power. (2:43)

To those attached to enjoyment and power, their minds drawn away by this speech, is not granted steady insight in meditation. (2:44)

The three gunas are the domains of the Vedas. Be free from the triad of the gunas, indifferent to the pairs of opposites, eternally established in reality, free from thoughts of getting and keeping, and established in the Self. (2:45)

For the wise Brahmin with true knowledge, a great deal in all the Vedas are of as much value as a well when there is a flood all around. (2:46)

Your authority is for action alone, never to its fruits at any time. Never should the fruits of action be your motive; and never should there be attachment to inaction in you. (2:47)

Steadfast in yoga, perform actions abandoning attachment, being indifferent to success or failure. It is said that such evenness of mind is yoga. (2:48)

Action is inferior by far to buddhi yoga. Seek refuge in enlightenment; pitiable are those who are motivated by action's fruit. (2:49)

He who abides in the buddhi casts off here in this world both good and evil deeds. Therefore, yoke yourself to yoga. Yoga is skill in action. (2:50)

Those who are truly established in the buddhi, the wise ones, having abandoned the fruits of action, freed from the bondage of rebirth, go to the place that is free from pain. (2:51)

When your buddhi crosses beyond the mire of delusion, then you shall be disgusted with the to-be-heard and what has been heard. (2:52)

When your buddhi stands, fixed in deep meditation, unmoving, disregarding the Vedic ritual-centered perspective, then you will attain yoga (union). (2:53)

Higher mind

Arjuna said:

What is the description of him who is steady of insight, of him who is steadfast in deep meditation, of him who is steady in thought? How does he speak? How does he sit? How does he move about? (2:54)

The Holy Lord said:

When he leaves behind all the desires of the mind, contented in the Self by the Self, then he is said to be steady in wisdom. (2:55)

He whose mind is not agitated in misfortunes, freed from desire for pleasures, from whom passion, fear and anger have departed, steady in thought–such a man is said to be a sage. (2:56)

He who is without desire in all situations, encountering this or that, pleasant or unpleasant, not rejoicing or disliking–his wisdom stands firm. (2:57)

And when he withdraws completely the senses from the objects of the senses, as the tortoise draws in its limbs, his wisdom is established firmly. (2:58)

Sense-objects turn away from the abstinent, yet the taste for them remains. But the taste also turns away from him who has seen the Supreme. (2:59)

The troubling senses forcibly carry away the mind of even the striving man of wisdom. (2:60)

Restraining all these senses, he should sit in yoga, intent on me. Surely, he whose senses are controlled–his consciousness stands steadfast and firm. (2:61)

For a man dwelling on the objects of the senses, attachment to them is born. From attachment desire is born. And from thwarted desire anger is born. (2:62)

From anger arises delusion; from delusion, loss of memory; from loss of memory, destruction of intelligence. From destruction of intelligence one is lost. (2:63)

However, with attraction and aversion eliminated, even though moving amongst objects of sense, by self-restraint the self-controlled attains tranquility. (2:64)

In tranquility the cessation of all sorrows is produced for him. Truly, for the tranquil-minded the buddhi immediately becomes steady. (2:65)

For the undisciplined there is no wisdom, no meditation. For him who does not meditate there is no peace or happiness. (2:66)

When the mind is led about by the wandering senses, it carries away the understanding like the wind carries away a ship on the waters. (2:67)

The intelligent, buddhic awareness of him whose senses are withdrawn from the objects of the senses on all sides will be found firmly established. (2:68)

The man of restraint is awake in what is night for all beings. That in which all beings are awake is night for the sage who truly sees. (2:69)

Like the ocean, which becomes filled yet remains unmoved and stands still as the waters enter it, he whom all desires enter and who remains unmoved attains peace—not so the man who is full of desire. (2:70)

He who abandons all desires attains peace, acts free from longing, indifferent to possessions and free from egotism. (2:71)

This is the divine state. Having attained this, he is not deluded. Fixed in it even at the time of death, he attains Brahmanirvana. (2:72)

Om Tat Sat

Thus in the Upanishads of the glorious Bhagavad Gita, the science of the Eternal, the scripture of Yoga, the dialogue between Sri Krishna and Arjuna, ends the second discourse entitled: Sankhya Yoga.

Chapter Three

THE YOGA OF ACTION

Arjuna said:

If it is your conviction that knowledge is better than action, then why do you urge me to engage in this terrible action? (3:1)

With speech that seems equivocal you confuse my mind. Tell me surely this one thing: How should I attain the highest good? (3:2)

The Holy Lord said:

In this world there is a two-fold path taught by me long ago: knowledge, the yoga of the Sankhyas, and action, the yoga of the yogis. (3:3)

Not by abstaining from actions does a man attain the state beyond action, and not by mental renunciation alone does he approach to perfection. (3:4)

Truly, no one for even a moment exists without doing action. Each person is compelled to perform action, even against his will, by the gunas born of prakriti. (3:5)

Not a case of not engaging the senses, more control them, not them controlling you.

He who restrains action's organs while yet revolving in his mind thoughts of objects of the senses, is deluded, a hypocrite. (3:6)

He who by the mind controls the senses, and yet is unattached while engaging action's organs in action, is superior. (3:7)

Perform your duty, for action is far better than non-action. Even maintaining your body cannot be done without action. (3:8)

The world is bound by the actions not done for sake of sacrifice. Hence for sacrifice you should act without attachment. (3:9)

In the beginning along with mankind Prajapati created sacrifice and said: "By this shall you increase: this shall be the granter of desires. (3:10)

"May you foster the gods by this, and may the gods then foster you. Then, each the others fostering, you shall attain the highest welfare. (3:11)

"The gods, fostered by sacrifice, will give you desired enjoyments. But he who enjoys the gods' gifts without offering to them is a thief." (3:12)

The good who eat the sacrificial remains are freed from all evils. The wicked eat their own evil who cook food only for themselves. (3:13)

From food all beings are produced, and from rain all food is produced. From sacrifice there comes down rain. From action is born sacrifice. (3:14)

Understand that action arises from Brahma, Brahma arises from the Imperishable. Hence the all-pervading Brahma is eternally established in sacrifice. (3:15)

He who here on the earth turns not the wheel thus set in motion, lives full of sense delights, maliciously and uselessly. (3:16)

He who is content only in the Self, who is satisfied in the Self, who is pleased only in the Self: for him there is no need to act. (3:17)

He has no purpose at all in action or in non-action, and he has no need of anyone for any purpose whatsoever. (3:18)

Therefore, constantly unattached perform that which is your duty. Indeed by unattached action man attains the Supreme. (3:19)

Indeed, perfection was attained through action alone by King Janaka and others. For the maintenance of the world, as an example you should act. (3:20)

Whatever the best of men does–this and that–thus other men do. Whatever the standard that he sets, that is what the world shall follow. (3:21)

I have no duty whatsoever in the three worlds, nor anything that must be attained, nevertheless I engage in action. (3:22)

Indeed, if I did not tirelessly engage at all in action, then mankind everywhere would follow my example. (3:23)

If I did not perform action these worlds would perish, and I would be the cause of confusion. I would destroy these people. (3:24)

As the unwise act, attached to action, so the wise should act, unattached, intending to maintain the welfare of the world. (3:25)

One should not unsettle the minds of the ignorant attached

to action. The wise should cause them to enjoy all actions, himself engaged in their performance. (3:26)

In all situations actions are performed by the gunas of Prakriti. Those with ego-deluded mind think: "I am the doer." (3:27)

But he who knows the truth about the gunas and action thinks: "The gunas act in the gunas." Thinking thus, he is not attached. (3:28)

Those deluded by the gunas of prakriti are attached to the actions of the gunas. The knower of the whole truth should not disturb the foolish of partial knowledge. (3:29)

Renouncing all actions in me, intent on the Supreme Spirit, free from desire and "mine," free from the "fever" of delusion and grief: fight! (3:30)

Those who constantly follow this teaching of mine, full of faith, not opposing it, they are released from the bondage of their actions. (3:31)

But those opposing and not practicing my teaching, confusing all knowledge, know them to be lost and mindless. (3:32)

One acts according to one's own prakriti—even the wise man does so. Beings follow their own prakriti; what will restraint accomplish? (3:33) ↓ Energy

Attraction and aversion are inherent in the contact of the senses with sense-objects. One should not come under the power of these two—they are indeed his enemies. (3:34)

Better is one's swadharma, though deficient, than the swadharma of another well performed. Better is death in one's own swadharma. The swadharma of another brings danger. (3:35)

Arjuna said:

Then by what is a man impelled to commit evil, against his own will, as if urged by some force? (3:36)

The Holy Lord said:

This force is desire and anger born of the rajo-guna, the great consumer and of great evil. Know this to be the enemy. (3:37)

As fire is enveloped by smoke, as mirrors are covered by dust, as wombs cover embryos, in the same way (3:38)

Knowledge is covered by this, the constant enemy of the wise, having the form of desire which is like insatiable fire. (3:39)

The senses, mind, and intellect are said to be its abode. With these it deludes the embodied one by veiling his innate wisdom. (3:40)

Therefore, controlling the senses at the outset, kill this evil being, which destroys ordinary knowledge and supreme knowledge. (3:41)

They say that the senses are superior to the body, the mind is superior to the senses, the intellect is superior to the mind. And much superior to the intellect is (3:42)

The supreme intelligence. Having learned this, sustaining the lower self by the higher Self, kill this difficult-to-encounter enemy which has the form of desire. (3:43)

Om Tat Sat

Thus in the Upanishads of the glorious Bhagavad Gita, the science of the Eternal, the scripture of Yoga, the dialogue between Sri Krishna and Arjuna, ends the third discourse entitled: The Yoga of Action.

Chapter Four

THE YOGA OF WISDOM

The Holy Lord said:

This eternal yoga I taught to Vivaswat, Vivaswat taught it to Manu, and Manu taught it to Ikshwaku. (4:1)

Thus, handed down in succession, the royal seers knew it. After a long lapse of time, this yoga was lost here on earth. (4:2)

This ancient yoga is today declared by me to you because you are my devotee and friend. This secret is supreme indeed. (4:3)

Arjuna said:

Your birth was later, and Vivaswat's birth was earlier. How then should I understand that you taught this in the beginning? (4:4)

The Holy Lord said:

Many of my births have passed away, and also yours. I know them all; you do not know them. (4:5)

Although birthless and imperishable, although the Lord of all beings, controlling my own prakriti, I come into manifested being by my own power of maya. (4:6)

Whenever dharma decreases and there is the arising of adharma, then do I manifest myself. (4:7)

For protection of the righteous and destruction of evildoers, for the establishing of dharma, I manifest myself from age to age. (4:8)

He who knows in truth my divine birth and action, leaving the body is not born again: he comes to me. (4:9)

Free from greed, fear and anger, absorbed in me, holding fast to me, purified by knowledge-based tapasya, many have attained my state of being. (4:10)

In whatever way men resort to me do I thus reward them. It is my path which men follow everywhere. (4:11)

Longing for success in action, in this world men sacrifice to the gods because success from such action is quickly attained in the human world. (4:12)

The fourfold caste was created by me, based on guna and on karma. Though I am the creator thereof, know me to be the eternal non-doer. (4:13)

Actions do not taint me, nor is desire for action's fruit in me. He who thus comprehends me is not bound by actions. (4:14)

Knowing thus, the ancient seekers for liberation performed action. Do you, therefore, perform action as did the ancients in earlier times. (4:15)

What is action? What is inaction? Even the poet-sages were bewildered regarding this matter. This action shall I explain to you, which having known you shall be freed from evil. (4:16)

Truly the nature of action, of wrong action and of non-action is to be known. The path of action is difficult to understand. (4:17)

He who perceives inaction in action and action in inaction—such a man is wise among men, steadfast in yoga and doing all action. (4:18)

Whose undertakings are devoid of plan and desire for results, whose actions are consumed in the fire of knowledge–him the wise call wise. (4:19)

Having abandoned attachment for action's fruit, always content, not dependent on anything even when acting, he truly does nothing at all. (4:20)

Acting with the body alone, without wish, with thought and lower self restrained, abandoning all acquisitiveness, though acting he incurs no fault. (4:21)

Content with what comes unbidden, beyond the pairs of opposites and free from envy, the same in success or failure, even though acting, he is not bound. (4:22)

The karma of one who is free from attachment, whose thought is established in knowledge, undertaking action for sacrifice, is wholly dissolved. (4:23)

Brahman is the offering, Brahman is the oblation poured out by Brahman into the fire of Brahman. Brahman is to be attained by him who always sees Brahman in action. (4:24)

Some yogis offer sacrifice to the gods alone, while others offer the Self as sacrifice unto the Self into the fire that is Brahman. (4:25)

Others offer senses such as hearing into the fires of restraint; others, sound; and others objects of the senses into the fire of the senses. (4:26)

Some offer all the actions of the senses and the functions of the life force (prana) into the fire of the yoga of self-restraint, which is enkindled by knowledge. (4:27)

Those whose sacrifices take the form of yoga offer material possessions and tapasya as sacrifices; while ascetics with stringent vows offer self-analysis and knowledge as sacrifice. (4:28)

Some offer inhalation into exhalation, and exhalation into inhalation, restraining the paths of inhalation and exhalation, intent upon control of the breath (pranayama). (4:29)

Others who have restricted their food offer the pranas into the pranas. All these are knowers of sacrifice whose wrongdoings have been annihilated through sacrifice. (4:30)

Eating the amrita of the sacrificial remains, they go to the Eternal Brahman. Even this world is not for the non-sacrificing–how then the other worlds? (4:31)

Sacrifices of many kinds are spread out before the face of Brahman. Know them all to be born from action. Knowing thus, you shall be liberated. (4:32)

Better than the sacrifice of material things is knowledge-sacrifice. All action without exception is fully contained in knowledge. (4:33)

Know that by prostrating yourself, by questioning and by serving them, the wise who have realized the truth will therefore instruct you in that knowledge. (4:34)

Know this, and you shall not again fall into delusion. By

this you shall come to see all creation in your Self and then in me. (4:35)

Even if you should be the most sinful among all the sinful, yet you would cross over all sin by the raft of knowledge alone. (4:36)

As the kindled fire reduces wood to ashes, in the same way the fire of knowledge reduces all karmas to ashes. (4:37)

No purifier equal to knowledge is found here in the world. He who is himself perfected in yoga in time finds knowledge in the Self. (4:38)

He who possesses faith attains knowledge. Devoted to that pursuit, restraining the senses, having attained knowledge he quickly attains supreme peace. (4:39)

The man who is ignorant and without faith, of a doubting nature, is ruined. Neither this world, nor the next, nor happiness is for the man of doubt. (4:40)

Action does not bind him whose actions are renounced in yoga, whose doubt is severed by knowledge, and who is self-possessed. (4:41)

Therefore, having severed with the sword of your own knowledge this doubt that proceeds from ignorance abiding in your heart, arise! Take refuge in yoga. (4:42)

Om Tat Sat

Thus in the Upanishads of the glorious Bhagavad Gita, the science of the Eternal, the scripture of Yoga, the dialogue between Sri Krishna and Arjuna, ends the fourth discourse entitled: The Yoga of Wisdom.

Chapter Five

THE YOGA OF RENUNCIATION OF ACTION

Arjuna said:

You praise renunciation of actions and again you praise karma yoga. Which one is the better of these two? Tell me definitely. (5:1)

The Holy Lord said:

Renunciation of action and karma yoga both lead to the highest happiness; of the two, however, karma yoga is superior to renunciation of action. (5:2)

He is a constant renouncer of action who neither hates nor desires, who is indifferent to the pairs of opposites–truly he is easily freed from bondage. (5:3)

"Sankhya and karma yoga are different," the childish declare– not the wise. If one is practiced correctly, that person finds the fruit of both. (5:4)

The realization that is attained by the followers of Sankhya is also attained by the followers of karma yoga. Sankhya and karma yoga are one. He who perceives this truly perceives. (5:5)

Indeed, renunciation is difficult to attain without karma yoga. The yoga-yoked sage quickly attains Brahman. (5:6)

Yoga-yoked, with the lower self purified, with the lower self subdued, whose senses are conquered, whose Self has become the Self of all beings–he is not tainted even when acting. (5:7)

"I do not do anything;" thus thinks the steadfast knower of truth while seeing, hearing, touching, smelling, eating, walking, sleeping, breathing, (5:8)

Speaking, releasing, and holding, opening and closing his eyes–convinced that it is the senses that move among the sense-objects. (5:9)

Offering actions to Brahman, having abandoned attachment, he acts untainted by evil as a lotus leaf is not wetted by water. (5:10)

Karma yogis perform action only with the body, mind, intellect, or the senses, forsaking attachment, performing action for self-purification. (5:11)

He who is steadfast, having abandoned action's fruit, attains lasting peace. He who is not steadfast, attached to action based on desire, is bound. (5:12)

Renouncing all actions with the mind, the embodied one sits happily as the ruler of the city of nine gates, not acting at all, nor causing action. (5:13)

The Lord does not create either means of action or action

itself in this world, nor the union of action with its fruit. On the other hand, the swabhava impels one to action. (5:14)

The Omnipresent takes note of neither demerit nor merit. Knowledge is enveloped by ignorance; as a result of that people are deluded. (5:15)

But those in whom this ignorance of the Self has been destroyed by knowledge–that knowledge of theirs, like the sun, reveals the Supreme Brahman. (5:16)

Those whose minds are absorbed in That, whose Selves are fixed on That, whose foundation is That, who hold That as the highest object, whose evils have been shaken off by knowledge, attain the ending of rebirth. (5:17)

The wise see the same Self in a wise and disciplined Brahmin, in a cow, in an elephant, in a dog, even in an eater of dogs. (5:18)

Even here on earth rebirth is conquered by those whose mind is established in evenness. Brahman is without fault and the same to all; therefore they are established in Brahman. (5:19)

One should not exult when encountering what is liked, and one should not be repulsed when encountering the disliked. With firm intellect, undeluded, the knower of Brahman is established in Brahman. (5:20)

He whose Self is unattached to external contacts, who finds happiness in the Self, whose Self is united to Brahman by yoga, reaches imperishable happiness. (5:21)

Truly, pleasures born of contact with the senses are wombs of pain, since they have a beginning and an end. The wise man is not satisfied with them. (5:22)

He who is able to endure here on earth, before liberation

from the body, the agitation that arises from desire and anger is steadfast, a happy man. (5:23)

He whose happiness is within, whose delight is within, whose illumination is within: that yogi, identical in being with Brahman, attains Brahmanirvana. (5:24)

The seers whose evils have been annihilated, whose doubts have been dispelled, whose inner being is mastered, who rejoice in the welfare of all beings, attain Brahmanirvana. (5:25)

Released from desire and anger, with thoughts controlled, those ascetics who know the Self find very near to them the bliss of Brahmanirvana. (5:26)

Excluding outside contacts, turning up the eyes toward the two brows, equalizing the inhalation and exhalation moving within the nostrils, (5:27)

With his senses, mind and intellect controlled, with liberation as his highest aim, free from desire, fear, and anger: such a one is forever free. (5:28)

Having known me, the enjoyer of the tapasyas offered as sacrifice, the mighty Lord of all the world and the friend of all creatures, he attains peace. (5:29)

Om Tat Sat

Thus in the Upanishads of the glorious Bhagavad Gita,
the science of the Eternal, the scripture of Yoga, the
dialogue between Sri Krishna and Arjuna, ends the
fifth discourse entitled: The Yoga of Renunciation of
Action.

Chapter Six

THE YOGA
OF MEDITATION

The Holy Lord said:

He who performs that action which is his duty, not caring for the action's fruit, is a renouncer and a yogi, not he without sacrificial fire and sacred rites. (6:1)

That which they call renunciation, know that to be yoga. Without renouncing selfish purpose no one whatever becomes a yogi. (6:2)

For the sage desirous of attaining yoga, action is said to be the means. For him who has already attained yoga, tranquility is said to be the means. (6:3)

When he is truly attached neither to sense objects nor to actions, and has renounced all purpose (sarva sankalpa), then he is said to have attained yoga. (6:4)

One should uplift oneself by the lower self; one should not degrade oneself. The lower self can truly be a friend of the lower self, and the lower self alone can be an enemy of the lower self. (6:5)

For him who has conquered himself by the lower self, the lower self is a friend. But for him who has not conquered himself, the lower self remains hostile, like an enemy. (6:6)

The highest Self of him who has conquered himself and is peaceful, is thus steadfast in cold, heat, pleasure, pain, honor and dishonor. (6:7)

The yogi who is satisfied with knowledge and discrimination, unchanging, with senses conquered, to whom a lump of clay, a stone and gold are the same, steadfast–is said to be in union. (6:8)

He is preeminent among men who is impartial to friend, associate and enemy, neutral among enemies and kinsmen, impartial also among the righteous and the unrighteous. (6:9)

The yogi should fix his awareness constantly on the Self, remaining in solitude, alone, with controlled mind and lower self, without desires or possessiveness. (6:10)

Establishing for himself a firm seat in a clean place, not too high and not too low, covered with kusha grass, an antelope skin and a cloth, (6:11)

There, having directed his mind to a single object, controlling thought and activity of the senses, sitting on the seat he should practice yoga for the purpose of self-purification. (6:12)

Holding the body, head and neck erect, motionless and steady, looking toward the origin of his nose and not looking around, (6:13)

With mind quieted, banishing fear, firm in the brahmachari's vow, controlling the mind, with thoughts fixed on me, steadfast, he should sit, devoted to me. (6:14)

Always disciplining himself thus, the yogi whose mind is subdued goes to the supreme peace of nirvana, and attains to union with me. (6:15)

Yoga is not eating too much, nor is it virtually not eating at all; not the habit of sleeping too much, and not keeping awake too much, either. (6:16)

For him who is moderate in food and diversion, disciplined in action, moderate in sleep and waking, yoga destroys all suffering. (6:17)

When he is absorbed in the Self alone, with mind controlled, free from longing, from all desires, then he is known to be steadfast. (6:18)

As a lamp in a windless place flickers not: to such is compared the yogi of controlled mind, performing the yoga of the Self. (6:19)

When the mind comes to rest, restrained by the practice of yoga, beholding the Self by the Self, he is content in the Self. (6:20)

He knows that endless joy which is apprehended by the buddhi beyond the senses; and established in that he does not deviate from the truth. (6:21)

Having attained this, he regards no other gain better than that, and established therein he is not moved by heaviest sorrow. (6:22)

Let this dissolution of union with pain be known as yoga. This yoga is to be practiced with determination, with an assured mind. (6:23)

Abandoning those desires whose origins lie in one's intention—all of them without exception—also completely restraining the many senses by the mind, (6:24)

With the buddhi firmly controlled, with the mind fixed on the Self, he should gain quietude by degrees. Let him not think of any extraneous thing whatever. (6:25)

Whenever the unsteady mind, moving here and there, wanders off, he should subdue and hold it back and direct it to the Self's control. (6:26)

The yogi whose mind is truly tranquil, with emotions calmed, free of evil, having become one with Brahman, attains the supreme happiness. (6:27)

Thus constantly engaging himself in the practice of yoga, that yogi, freed from evil, easily touching Brahman, attains boundless happiness. (6:28

He who is steadfast in yoga (yoga-yukta) at all times sees the Self present in all beings and all beings present in the Self. (6:29)

He who sees me everywhere, and sees all things in me—I am not lost to him, and he is not lost to me. (6:30)

He, established in unity, worships me dwelling in all things. Whatever be his mode of life, that yogi ever abides in me. (6:31)

He who judges pleasure or pain by the same standard everywhere that he applies unto himself, that yogi is deemed the highest. (6:32)

Arjuna said:
This yoga which is taught by you characterized by evenness

of mind, I do not see how it endures, owing to the mind's restlessness. (6:33)

The mind is truly unstable, troubling, strong and unyielding. I believe it is hard to control–as hard to control as the wind. (6:34)

The Holy Lord said:

Without doubt the mind is hard to control and restless; but through practice (abhyasa) and dispassion (vairagya) it is governed. (6:35)

I agree that yoga is difficult to attain by him whose lower self is uncontrolled; but by him whose lower self is controlled by striving by right means, it is possible to attain it. (6:36)

Arjuna said:

One who has faith but is uncontrolled, whose mind has fallen away from yoga without reaching perfection in yoga–which way does he go? (6:37)

Is he not lost like a dissolving cloud, fallen from both worlds– here and hereafter, having no solid ground, confused on the path of Brahman? (6:38)

You are able to completely remove this my doubt. Other than you there is no one who can dispel this doubt. (6:39)

The Holy Lord said:

Truly there is no loss for him either here on earth or in heaven. No one who does good goes to misfortune. (6:40)

Attaining the worlds of the meritorious, having dwelt there

for countless years, he who has fallen from yoga is reborn in a happy and illustrious family. (6:41)

Or else he may be born into a family of wise yogis. Truly, a birth such as that is more difficult to obtain in this world. (6:42)

There he regains the knowledge he acquired in his former incarnation, and strives from thence once more toward perfection. (6:43)

Truly, without his willing it his previous practice impels him on the yogic path. He who just desires to know about yoga goes beyond the Vedas. (6:44)

By persevering effort and mastery, the totally purified yogi, perfected through many births, reaches the Supreme Goal. (6:45)

The yogi is superior to ascetics, and considered superior to jnanis and superior to those engaged in Vedic rituals. Therefore be a yogi. (6:46)

Of all the yogis, he who has merged his inner Self in me and honors me, full of faith, I consider him the most devoted to me. (6:47)

Om Tat Sat

Thus in the Upanishads of the glorious Bhagavad Gita, the science of the Eternal, the scripture of Yoga, the dialogue between Sri Krishna and Arjuna, ends the sixth discourse entitled: The Yoga of Meditation.

Chapter Seven

THE YOGA OF WISDOM AND REALIZATION

The Holy Lord said:

With mind absorbed in me, practicing yoga, taking refuge in me, hear how without doubt you shall know me completely. (7:1)

To you I shall explain in full this knowledge, along with realization, which being known, nothing further remains to be known in this world. (7:2)

Of thousands of human beings scarcely anyone at all strives for perfection, and of those adept in that striving, scarcely anyone knows me in truth. (7:3)

Earth, water, fire, air, ether, mind, intellect and ego-principle: these are the eight divisions of my prakriti. (7:4)

This is my lower prakriti, yet know my higher prakriti as consisting of all jivas, by which this world is sustained. (7:5)

Realize that these two prakritis are the wombs of all beings. Of this entire world I am the origin and the dissolution. (7:6)

Than me there is nothing higher. All this creation is strung on me like pearls on a thread. (7:7)

I am the taste within water, the radiance of the moon and the sun; Om in all the Vedas, the sound in the ether and the manhood in men. (7:8)

I am the pure fragrance in the earth, and the brilliance within fire; the life in all beings, and the tapasya of ascetics. (7:9)

Know that I am the eternal seed of all beings, the intelligence of the intelligent, and the splendor of the splendid. (7:10)

I am the strength of the strong, free from desire and passion. I am the desire in beings that is according to dharma. (7:11)

Know that sattwic, rajasic and tamasic states of being proceed from me. But I am not in them–they are in me. (7:12)

All this world is deluded by the three states produced by the gunas. It does not perceive me, who am higher than these and eternal. (7:13)

Truly this maya of mine made of the gunas is difficult to go beyond. Verily only those who attain me shall pass beyond this maya. (7:14)

Evil-doers, the lowest of men, bereft of knowledge by maya, do not seek me, being attached to (existing within) a demonic mode of existence. (7:15)

Among the virtuous, four kinds seek me: the distressed, the seekers of knowledge, the seekers of wealth and the wise. (7:16)

Of them, the wise man, ever united, devoted to the One, is pre-eminent. Exceedingly dear am I to the man of wisdom, and he is dear to me. (7:17)

All these indeed are exalted, but I see the man of wisdom as my very Self. He, with mind steadfast, abides in me, the Supreme Goal. (7:18)

At the end of many births the wise man takes refuge in me. He knows: All is Vasudeva. How very rare is that great soul. (7:19)

Those whose knowledge has been stolen away by various desires resort to other gods, following various religious practices, impelled thus by their own natures. (7:20)

Whoever wishes to worship whatever form with faith, on him I bestow immovable faith. (7:21)

He who, endowed with this faith, desires to propitiate that form, receives from it his desires because their fulfillment has been decreed by me. (7:22)

But temporary is the fruit for those of small understanding. To the gods go the worshippers of the gods. Those who worship me come unto me. (7:23)

Though I am unmanifest, the unintelligent think me entered into manifestation, not knowing my higher being which is imperishable and unsurpassed. (7:24)

Veiled by Yogamaya, I am not manifest to all. This deluded world perceives me not who am unborn and imperishable. (7:25)

I know the departed beings and the living, and those who are yet to be, but none whatsoever knows me. (7:26)

By desire and aversion rising up through duality's delusion, at birth all beings fall into delusion. (7:27)

But those whose wrongdoing has come to an end, whose actions are righteous, freed from the delusions of the pairs of opposites–they worship me with firm resolve. (7:28)

Those who strive toward freedom from old age and dying, taking refuge in me, know Brahman totally, and know the Self and karma perfectly. (7:29)

Those who know me as the Primal Being and the Primal God, as well as the Primal Sacrifice, they know me with steadfast thought also at the time of death. (7:30)

Om Tat Sat

Thus in the Upanishads of the glorious Bhagavad Gita, the science of the Eternal, the scripture of Yoga, the dialogue between Sri Krishna and Arjuna, ends the seventh discourse entitled: The Yoga of Wisdom and Realization.

Chapter Eight

THE YOGA OF IMPERISHABLE BRAHMAN

Arjuna said:

O Supreme Spirit: What is Brahman? What is the Primal Self? What is action? What is the Primal Being? What is the Primal God? (8:1)

What, and in what way, is the Primal Sacrifice here in this body? And how are you to be known at the time of death by the self-controlled ones? (8:2)

The Holy Lord said: ↑ Sacrifce

The Imperishable is the Supreme Brahman. Its dwelling in each individual body is called the Primal Self; the offering in sacrifice which causes the genesis and support of beings is called Karma. (8:3)

Primal Being is perishable existence; the Primal God is the

Supreme Divine Being; and I myself am the Primal Sacrifice. (8:4)

At the time of death he who remembers me while giving up the body attains my Being–of this there is no doubt. (8:5)

Moreover, whatever he fixes his mind on when he gives up the body at the end, to that he goes. Always he becomes that. (8:6)

Therefore at all times remember me, and fight with your mind and intellect fixed on me. Thus without doubt you shall come to me. (8:7)

With mind made steadfast by yoga, which turns not to anything else, to the Divine Supreme Spirit he goes, meditating on him. (8:8)

He who meditates on the Seer, the Ancient, the Ruler, subtler than the atom, Support of all, whose form is inconceivable and radiant like the sun and beyond darkness, (8:9)

At the time of death with mind unmoving, endowed with devotion and yoga power, having made the prana enter between the eyebrows, he goes to the Divine Supreme Spirit. (8:10)

That which the knowers of the Veda call the Eternal, which the ascetics free from passion enter, desiring which they live the life of brahmacharya, that path I shall explain unto you briefly. (8:11)

Closing all the doors of the body, confining the mind in the heart, drawing his prana into the head, established in yoga concentration, (8:12)

Uttering Om, the single-syllabled Brahman, meditating on me, departing thus from his body, he attains the Goal Supreme. (8:13)

He who thinks of me constantly, whose mind never goes elsewhere, for him, the constantly-united yogi, I am easy to attain. (8:14)

Coming to me, those great souls who have reached the highest perfection do not incur rebirth in this world, which is, the impermanent home of suffering. (8:15)

The worlds up to Brahma's realm are subject to rebirth's return, but for him who attains to me there is no more rebirth. (8:16)

They know the true day and night who know Brahma's Day a thousand yugas long and Brahma's Night a thousand yugas long. (8:17)

At the approach of Brahma's Day, all manifested things come forth from the unmanifest, and then return to that at Brahma's Night. (8:18)

Helpless, the same host of beings being born again and again merge at the approach of the Night and emerge at the dawn of Day. (8:19)

But there exists, higher than the unmanifested, another unmanifested Eternal which does not perish when all beings perish. (8:20)

This unmanifest is declared to be the imperishable, which is called the Supreme Goal, attaining which they return not. This is my supreme abode. (8:21)

This is the Supreme Being, attained by one-pointed devotion alone, within which all beings do dwell, by which all this is pervaded. (8:22)

Now I shall tell you of the times in which the yogis, departing at the time of death, return or do not return. (8:23)

Fire, light, daytime, the bright lunar fortnight, the six months of the sun's north path: departing then the Brahman-knowers go to Brahman. (8:24)

Smoke, nighttime, the dark fortnight, the six months of the sun's south path: thereby attaining the lunar light, the yogi returns again. (8:25)

Truly these two light and dark paths the world thinks to be eternal. By one he goes to non-return; by the other he returns again. (8:26)

No yogi who knows these two paths is confused. Therefore at all times be steadfast in yoga. (8:27)

Whatever meritorious fruit is declared to accrue from study or recitation of the Vedas, sacrifice, tapasya, and almsgiving–beyond all these goes the yogi who knows the two paths; and he attains to the supreme, primeval Abode. (8:28)

Om Tat Sat

Thus in the Upanishads of the glorious Bhagavad Gita, the science of the Eternal, the scripture of Yoga, the dialogue between Sri Krishna and Arjuna, ends the eighth discourse entitled: The Yoga of Imperishable Brahman.

Chapter Nine

THE YOGA OF THE ROYAL SCIENCE AND ROYAL SECRET

The Holy Lord said:

To you who do not disbelieve I shall declare this most secret knowledge combined with realization, which having known you shall be free from evil. (9:1)

Royal knowledge, royal secret, this the supreme purifier, readily understood, dharmic, pleasant to practice, eternal. (9:2)

Those who have no faith in this dharma, without attaining me are reborn in the realm of death and samsara. (9:3)

All this world is pervaded by me in my unmanifest aspect. All beings dwell within me, but I do not dwell within them. (9:4)

And yet beings do not dwell within me: behold my Divine Yoga. Sustaining beings and yet not dwelling in them, I myself cause all beings to come into manifestation. (9:5)

As mighty winds move everywhere, yet always dwell in the

ether, know that even so do all beings dwell within me. (9:6)

At the end of a kalpa, all beings merge into my Prakriti: at the beginning of another kalpa, I myself send them forth. (9:7)

Resting on my Prakriti, I send forth again and again this entire multitude of beings, helpless under Prakriti's power. (9:8)

And these acts do not bind me, sitting as one apart, indifferent and unattached in these actions. (9:9)

With me as overseer Prakriti produces both the animate and the inanimate; because of this the world revolves. (9:10)

The deluded despise me dwelling in human form, not knowing of my higher being as the Great Lord of all beings. (9:11)

Those of vain hopes, vain deeds, vain knowledge, without intelligence, abide in the delusive nature of rakshasas and asuras. (9:12)

But those great souls that abide in their divine nature, worship me single-mindedly, knowing me as the eternal Origin of beings. (9:13)

Always glorifying me and striving with firm vows, bowing to me with devotion, always steadfast, they worship me. (9:14)

And others, sacrificing by the sacrifice of knowledge, worship me as One and Manifold, variously manifested, omniscient. (9:15)

I am the ritual, I am the sacrifice, I am the offering, I am the herb, I am the mantra, I am the ghee, I am the fire, and the pouring out into the fire. (9:16)

I am the Father and Mother of this world, Establisher, Grandfather, the object of knowledge, the Purifier, the Omkara (Om), the Rig, Sama and Yajur Vedas. (9:17)

I am the Goal, the Sustainer, the Lord, the Witness, the Abode, the Refuge, the Friend, the Origin, the Dissolution, the Foundation, the Treasure house and the Eternal Seed. (9:18)

As the sun I radiate heat; I withhold and send forth rain; I am immortality and death; being and non-being am I. (9:19)

The knowers of the three Vedas, the Soma drinkers, purified of sins, worshipping by sacrifices, seek the goal of heaven; they, the meritorious, attaining the world of Indra, enjoy divine, heavenly pleasures of the gods. (9:20)

Having enjoyed the vast heaven-world, with merit exhausted, they reenter the world of mortals. Thus, carrying out the injunctions of the three Vedas, desiring objects of desire, going and coming from birth to birth, they obtain them. (9:21)

Those men who single-mindedly direct their thoughts to me, worship me. For them who are constantly steadfast I bestow what they lack and preserve that which they possess. (9:22)

Even those who with devotion worship other gods also worship me, though with a mistaken approach.* (9:23)

Truly I am the Enjoyer and Lord of all sacrifices; but because they do not know me in truth they fall back into rebirth in this world. (9:24)

Those who are devoted to the gods go to the gods. Those who are devoted to the ancestors go to the ancestors. Those who are devoted to the spirits go to the spirits. Those who are devoted to me surely come to me. (9:25)

Whoever offers to me with devotion a leaf, a flower, a fruit, or water, I accept that offering of devotion from him whose heart is pure. (9:26)

Whatever you do, whatever you eat, whatever you offer in sacrifice, whatever you give, whatever tapasya you practice, do that as an offering to me. (9:27)

Thus shall you be freed from the bonds of actions producing both good and evil fruits. Steadfast in the yoga of renunciation and totally liberated, you shall come to me. (9:28)

I am the same to all beings. There is no one who is disliked or dear to me. But they who worship me with devotion are in me, and I am also in them. (9:29)

If even an evildoer worships me single-heartedly, he should be considered righteous, for truly he has rightly resolved. (9:30)

Quickly he becomes a virtuous soul and goes to everlasting peace. Understand: no devotee of me is ever lost. (9:31)

Truly, those who take refuge in me even though they be from wicked origins, women,** Vaishyas or Shudras, they also attain the Supreme Goal. (9:32)

How much more easily, then, the holy Brahmins and devoted royal (kshatriya) sages. Having come to this impermanent and unhappy world, devote yourself to me. (9:33)

With mind fixed on me, devoted, worshipping, bow down to me. Thus steadfast, with me as your supreme aim, you shall come to me. (9:34)

* The words "with a mistaken approach" is the best I can do with avidhipurvakam. It literally means "not according to the rules" or even "without/outside the rules." The idea seems to be that these people do not know or understand how to worship God correctly

because they do not know or understand the nature of God. Other possible terms–ignorantly, incorrectly, mistakenly, improperly, inappropriately, inappositely, inaptly, ineptly, haphazardly, irregularly–either express a value judgment or add an extra meaning or attitude the Sanskrit does not include.

** At the time of Krishna, and even today in India, some people, denying the truth of the Self, claim that only Brahmin and Kshatriya males can attain liberation. Krishna denies this.

Om Tat Sat

Thus in the Upanishads of the glorious Bhagavad Gita, the science of the Eternal, the scripture of Yoga, the dialogue between Sri Krishna and Arjuna, ends the ninth discourse entitled: The Yoga of the Royal Science and Royal Secret.

Chapter Ten

THE YOGA
OF DIVINE GLORIES

The Holy Lord said:

Once more hear from me the supreme word which I speak to you, who are beloved, with the desire for your welfare. (10:1)

Neither the multitude of gods nor the great seers (rishis) know my origin. In truth I am the universal source of the gods and the great seers. (10:2)

He who knows me as birthless and beginningless, the mighty Lord of the world–he among mortals is undeluded and freed from all evils. (10:3)

Intelligence, knowledge, non-delusion, forbearance, truthfulness, self-restraint, equanimity, happiness, suffering, birth, death, fear, and fearlessness, (10:4)

Non-injury, impartiality, contentment, tapasya, almsgiving, both good repute and ill repute: these manifold conditions of beings arise from me alone. (10:5)

In the past the ancient Seven Great Rishis and Four Manus, from whom have sprung these earthly beings, originated from me, born of my mind. (10:6)

He who knows in truth this my manifested glory and power is united with me by unwavering yoga–of this there is no doubt. (10:7)

I am the origin of all; from me everything proceeds–thinking thus, the wise, endowed with meditation, worship me. (10:8)

With minds and lives intent on me, enlightening one another, and speaking of me constantly, they are content and rejoice in me. (10:9)

To them, the constantly steadfast, worshipping me with affection, I bestow the buddhi yoga by which they come to me. (10:10)

Out of compassion for them, I, abiding in their own Selves, destroy the darkness born of ignorance by the shining lamp of knowledge. (10:11)

Arjuna said:

You are the Supreme Brahman, the Supreme Abode, the Supreme Purifier, the Divine Eternal Spirit, the First God, the Birthless and All-pervading. (10:12)

Thus do all the sages declare you: the Divine Sage Narada, Asita, Devala, and Vyasa. And you yourself say it to me. (10:13)

All this which you say to me I believe is true. Truly, Lord God (Bhagavan), neither the gods nor the demons know your manifestation. (10:14)

For you alone know yourself by yourself, O you, the

Purushottama: bestowing welfare on all beings, Lord of Beings, God of gods, Lord of the universe. (10:15)

Please describe completely your divine self-manifestations by which manifestations you pervade the worlds and abide in them. (10:16)

How may I know you, O Yogi, constantly meditating on you? And in what aspects of your Being are you to be thought of by me, O Bhagavan? (10:17)

Explain to me further in detail your powers and manifestations. I am never satiated with hearing your amrita-like words. (10:18)

The Holy Lord said:

Listen! I shall recount to you my truly divine self-manifestations—only the most prominent because there is no end to my extent. (10:19)

I am the Self abiding in the heart of all beings; I am the beginning, the middle and the end of all beings as well. (10:20)

Of the Adityas I am Vishnu; of luminaries the radiant Sun; of the Maruts I am Marichi; among the stars I am the Moon. (10:21)

Of the Vedas I am the Sama Veda; of the gods I am Indra; of the senses I am the mind; in all beings I am consciousness. (10:22)

Of the Rudras I am Shankara (Shiva); of the yakshas and v* I am Kubera; of the Vasus I am Pavaka [Agni]; and of mountains I am Meru. (10:23)

Of priests know me to be the chief, Brihaspati; of commanders

of armies I am Skanda; of bodies of water I am the ocean. (10:24)
Of the great Rishis I am Bhrigu; of words I am Om; of
sacrifices I am japa; of immovables I am the Himalayas. (10:25)
Of trees I am the ashwattha; of divine seers I am Narada; of
the gandharvas I am Chitraratha; among the siddhas I am the
sage Kapila. (10:26)
Of horses know me to be Uchchaishravas who was produced
from the amrita; of princely elephants I am Airavata; and among
men I am the king. (10:27)
Of weapons I am the Thunderbolt of Indra; of cows I am
Kamadhenu; of procreators I am Kamadeva; of serpents I am
Vasuki. (10:28)
Of Nagas I am Ananta; of water beings Varuna; of Ancestors
I am Aryaman; of subduers I am Yama. (10:29)
Of Daityas I am Prahlada; among measurers I am Time; of
animals I am the lion; of birds I am Garuda. (10:30)
Of purifiers I am the wind; of warriors I am Rama; of sea
creatures I am the dolphin; of rivers I am the Ganges. (10:31)
Of creations I am the beginning, the middle and the end;
of knowledge, the knowledge of the Self; of debaters I am logic.
(10:32)
Of letters I am the letter A; of compounds I am the dual; I
am infinite Time; I am the Sustainer, the Omniscient. (10:33)
I am all-devouring death and the origin of those events that
are to be. Among feminine qualities I am fame, prosperity, speech,
memory, mental vigor, courage and endurance. (10:34)
Of chants I am the Brihatsaman; of meters I am Gayatri;
of months I am Margashirsha; of seasons I am Spring. (10:35)

I am the gambling skill of the fraudulent, the splendor of the splendorous; I am victory and effort; I am the sattwa of the sattwic. (10:36)

Of the Vrishnis I am Krishna; of the Pandavas I am Arjuna; of the sages I am Vyasa; of the poets I am Ushanas. (10:37)

I am the power of rulers, I am the strategy of the ambitious, of secrets I am silence, the knowledge of knowers am I. (10:38)

Also I am that which is the seed of all beings. There is nothing that could exist without existing through me–neither animate nor inanimate. (10:39)

There is no end to my divine manifestations. But this has been declared by me to exemplify the extent of my manifestations. (10:40)

Whatever is glorious or prosperous or powerful, in every instance understand that it springs from but a fraction of my radiant Power. (10:41)

But what is this extensive knowledge to you? I ever support this whole world by just one portion of myself. (10:42)

* In this verse, "yakshas and rakshasas" refers to the benevolent, semidivine beings.

Om Tat Sat

Thus in the Upanishads of the glorious Bhagavad Gita, the science of the Eternal, the scripture of Yoga, the dialogue between Sri Krishna and Arjuna, ends the tenth discourse entitled: The Yoga of Divine Glories.

Chapter Eleven

THE YOGA OF THE VISION OF THE COSMIC FORM

Arjuna said:

As a kindness to me you spoke the Supreme Secret that is known as the Supreme Self. By this my confusion is gone. (11:1)

The origin and dissolution of beings has been heard by me in detail from you, and your eternal greatness. (11:2)

Thus, as you have described yourself, O Supreme Lord, I wish to behold your Ishwara Form, O Purushottama. (11:3)

If you think it is possible for me to see it, O Lord of Yogis, then show to me your eternal Self. (11:4)

The Holy Lord said:

Behold my forms a hundredfold–rather, a thousandfold–various, divine, and of many colors and shapes. (11:5)

Behold the Adityas, the Vasus, the Rudras, the two Ashwins, and the Maruts. Behold many wonders never seen before. (11:6)

See now present here in this my body the whole universe–both the animate and the inanimate–and whatever else you desire to see. (11:7)

But you are not able to see me with your own eyes. I give to you the divine eye: behold my Ishwara Power. (11:8)

Sanjaya said:

Then, having thus spoken, O King, Krishna, the Great Lord of Yoga, showed unto Arjuna his supreme Ishwara Form: (11:9)

With many mouths and eyes, with many wondrous aspects, with many divine ornaments, with many divine weapons upraised, (11:10)

Wearing divine garlands and clothing, with divine perfumes and ointments; embodying all wonders, the Infinite, Omniscient. (11:11)

If a thousand suns should rise together in the sky, such splendor would be like the brilliance of that Great Being. (11:12)

There, together in the body of the God of gods, Arjuna saw the entire universe present, though of many divisions. (11:13)

Then Arjuna, filled with astonishment and with his hair standing on end, bowing his head to the Divine Being, with joined palms said: (11:14)

Arjuna said:

O God, I behold all the gods and all kinds of beings together in your body: Lord Brahma seated upon the lotus, and all the rishis and celestial serpents. (11:15)

I see you in every direction in infinite form, with many

arms, stomachs, faces and eyes. Neither end, nor middle, nor beginning of you do I see, O Lord of All, whose form is the universe. (11:16)

I see you crowned, armed with a mace and a discus; a mass of radiance shining everywhere, very hard to look at, all around blazing like burning fire and the sun—beyond measure. (11:17)

You are the Unchanging, the supreme object of knowledge, you are the ultimate resting-place of all. You are the imperishable defender of Eternal Dharma, you are the Primal Purusha, I now realize. (11:18)

You are without beginning, middle or end, of infinite power, with innumerable arms; the sun and moon your eyes; blazing, consuming fire your mouth; consuming the universe with your brilliance. (11:19)

This space between heaven and earth and all the directions are filled by you alone. Seeing this, your marvelous and awesome form, the three worlds are trembling, O Exalted One. (11:20)

There, truly, into you enter the throngs of gods, some of which extol you in fear with joined palms, crying: "Hail!" The assemblages of great Rishis and Siddhas extol you with abundant praises. (11:21)

The Rudras, Adityas, Vasus, Sadhyas, and Vishwa-Devas, the two Ashwins, Maruts, Ushmapas, throngs of Gandharvas, Yakshas, Asuras, and Siddhas: all behold you, overcome. (11:22)

Having seen your great form with many mouths, eyes, many arms, many thighs and many feet, many stomachs, having many terrible tusks, the worlds are quaking, and so also am I. (11:23)

Truly, having seen you touching the sky, blazing, many-colored, with gaping mouths, with large and fiery eyes: I am trembling in my inmost heart, and find neither courage nor calm. (11:24)

Having seen your dreadful mouths, gaping with tusks, blazing like Pralaya-fires, I have no sense of direction or place of refuge. Have mercy, O Lord of Gods, Abode of the universe. (11:25)

And there all the sons of Dhritarashtra along with the throngs of kings, Bhishma, Drona, and Karna, with our chief warriors, (11:26)

Enter precipitately into your mouths, terrible, gaping with tusks and fearful to behold. Some are found sticking in the gaps between your teeth and some with their heads completely pulverized. (11:27)

As the torrents of many rivers flow towards the ocean, so these heroes of the world of men now enter into your flaming mouths. (11:28)

As moths precipitately rush into a blazing fire to destruction, in like manner so do these worlds also rush into your mouths to their destruction. (11:29)

You lick up and swallow all the worlds on every side with your flaming mouths. Filling the whole world with radiance, your fierce rays are consuming it, O Vishnu. (11:30)

Tell me who you are, you of terrible form. Salutations to you, O Best of Gods, be merciful. I desire to comprehend you, O Primal One. I wish to understand your intent. (11:31)

The Holy Lord said:
I am mighty world-destroying Time, here made manifest to annihilate the worlds. Even without you, none of the warriors

here arrayed within the hostile armies shall live. (11:32)

Therefore do you arise and acquire glory. Having conquered the enemies, enjoy thriving domain. These have already been struck down by me. Be merely an instrument. (11:33)

Drona, Bhishma, Jayadratha, Karna, and other battle heroes, already killed by me, do you kill. Do not hesitate. Fight. You shall conquer the adversaries in battle. (11:34)

Sanjaya said:

Having heard this speech of Krishna, Arjuna with joined palms and trembling, bowing down, addressed Krishna in a faltering voice, overwhelmed with fear. (11:35)

Arjuna said:

Rightly the world is delighted and rejoices in your renown. The demons, terrified, flee in all directions, and the throngs of siddhas bow to you in adoration. (11:36)

And why should they not bow to you, O Great One, Primal Creator greater than Brahma, Infinite Lord of Gods, Abode of the Universe, you the eternal, the truly existing, the non-existent, and That which is beyond both. (11:37)

You are the Primal God, the Ancient Purusha: you the supreme resting-place of all this universe. You are the knower, that which is to be known and the supreme dwelling state of consciousness and being. By you is the whole universe pervaded, O you of infinite forms. (11:38)

You are Vayu, Yama, Agni, Varuna, Chandra, Prajapati and the Great-grandfather, Brahma. I bow, yea, I bow to you a thousand times, again and again I bow, I bow to you. (11:39)

Salutation to you before and behind; salutation on every side, O All! You are infinite valor and boundless might. You pervade all–therefore you are All. (11:40)

Whatever I have said impetuously as in ordinary friendship: "O Krishna, O Yadava, O Comrade," unconscious of your greatness, through ignorance though with affection, (11:41)

And, as if joking, disrespectfully treated you in play, lying down, sitting or while eating, alone or with others, O Imperishable One, for that I ask pardon of you, O Boundless One. (11:42)

You are the Father of the world, of the animate and inanimate, you who are to be revered, you are the worshipful Guru. There is no one your equal in the three worlds. Who can excel you, O you of Incomparable Glory? (11:43)

Therefore, bowing down in prostration, I ask forgiveness of you, O Lord, who are worthy of honor. As a father to a son, a friend to a friend, a dear one to a beloved: O God, be merciful. (11:44)

I am delighted at having seen that which has never before been seen, and yet my mind trembles with fear. Show me in mercy, O Lord, your previous form, O Lord of gods, abode of the universe. (11:45)

I want to see you as before: wearing a crown, armed with a mace, holding a discus. Appear in that four-armed form, O you of a thousand arms, who are embodied in all the forms in the universe. (11:46)

The Holy Lord said:

By my grace toward you this supreme Form has been shown to you by my own power: this form of mine made of radiant splendor, universal, unbounded and primal, which has not been seen before by aught but you. (11:47)

Not by Vedic sacrifice or study, not by gifts, not by rites, nor by severe austerities can I be seen in such a form in the world of men, by any other than you. (11:48)

Be not afraid or bewildered, having seen this awesome form of mine. With your fears dispelled and with your heart gladdened, see once again this former form of mine. (11:49)

Sanjaya said:

Having thus spoken to Arjuna, Krishna showed once again his usual form. Thus the Great-souled One, having resumed his gentle, wondrous form, pacified the frightened one. (11:50)

Arjuna said:

Seeing your gentle human form, now I am composed and my mind is restored to normal. (11:51)

The Holy Lord said:

Difficult to see is this form of mine which you have seen. Even the gods ever long to behold this form. (11:52)

Not by Vedic study, not by tapasya, not by charitable gifts, and not by sacrifice can I be seen as you have seen me. (11:53)

By single-minded devotion alone can I be known and truly seen in this manner and entered into. (11:54)

He who engages in action, holding me as the highest aim, devoted, abandoning attachment, free from enmity to all beings, comes to me. (11:55)

Om Tat Sat

Thus in the Upanishads of the glorious Bhagavad Gita, the science of the Eternal, the scripture of Yoga, the dialogue between Sri Krishna and Arjuna, ends the eleventh discourse entitled: The Yoga of the Vision of the Cosmic Form.

Chapter Twelve

THE YOGA OF DEVOTION

Arjuna said:
The constantly steadfast who worship you with devotion,
and those who worship the eternal Unmanifest–which of them
has the better understanding of yoga? (12:1)

The Holy Lord said:
Those who are ever steadfast, who worship me, fixing their
minds on me, endowed with supreme faith, I consider them to
be the best versed in yoga. (12:2)

But those who worship the Imperishable, the Undefinable,
the Unmanifested, the All-pervading, Inconceivable, Unchanging, Unmoving, the Constant– (12:3)

Controlling all the senses, even-minded everywhere, happy
in the welfare of all beings–they attain to me also. (12:4)

Greater is the effort of those whose minds are set on the
Unmanifest, for the Unmanifest as a goal is truly difficult for
the embodied ones to reach. (12:5)

But those who, renouncing all actions in me, intent on me as the highest goal worship me, meditating on me with single-minded Yoga– (12:6)

Of those whose consciousness has entered into me, I am soon the deliverer from the ocean of mortal samsara. (12:7)

Keep your mind on me alone, causing your intellect to enter into me. Thenceforward, without doubt, you shall dwell in me. (12:8)

If you are unable to fix your mind on me steadily, then seek to attain me by the constant practice of yoga. (12:9)

If you are unable to practice yoga, be intent on acting for my sake. Even by performing actions for my sake, you shall attain perfection. (12:10)

If you are unable to do even this, then relying upon my yoga power, relinquishing all the fruits of action, act with self-restraint. (12:11)

Knowledge is indeed better than practice; meditation is superior to knowledge; renunciation of the fruit of action is better than meditation; peace immediately follows renunciation. (12:12)

He who hates no being, is friendly and compassionate, free from "mine," free from "I," the same in pain and pleasure, patient, (12:13)

The yogi who is always content, self-controlled and of firm resolve, whose mind and intellect are fixed on me, who is devoted to me–he is dear to me. (12:14)

He who agitates not the world, and whom the world agitates not, who is freed from joy, envy, fear and distress–he is dear to me. (12:15)

He who is indifferent, pure, capable, objective, free from anxiety, abandoning all undertakings, devoted to me–he is dear to me. (12:16)

He rejoices not, he hates not, he grieves not, he desires not, renouncing the agreeable and disagreeable, full of devotion–he is dear to me. (12:17)

The same to enemy and to friend, the same in honor and disgrace, in heat and cold, pleasure and pain, freed from attachment, (12:18)

The same in blame and praise, silent, content with anything whatever, not identifying with any place or abode, steady-minded, full of devotion–this man is dear to me. (12:19)

Those who honor this immortal dharma just described, endued with faith, deeming me the Goal Supreme, devoted–they are exceedingly dear to me. (12:20)

Om Tat Sat

Thus in the Upanishads of the glorious Bhagavad Gita,
the science of the Eternal, the scripture of Yoga, the
dialogue between Sri Krishna and Arjuna, ends the
twelfth discourse entitled: The Yoga of Devotion.

Chapter Thirteen

THE YOGA OF THE DISTINCTION BETWEEN THE FIELD AND THE KNOWER OF THE FIELD

Arjuna said:

Prakriti and Purusha, the Field and the Knower of the Field, knowledge, and that which should be known—I wish to know this, O Krishna.*

The Holy Lord said:

This body is called the Field, and he who knows this is called the Knower of the Field—so say the knowers of these things. (13:1)

And know me also to be the Knower of the Field in all fields. The knowledge of the Field and the Knower of the Field I consider to be *the* knowledge. (13:2)

The Field–what it is and of what kind, what its modifications are, whence they come and what are the Knower's powers, that hear from me in brief. (13:3)

This has been sung many times by the rishis in many sacred chants, in passages about Brahman, full of convincing reasoning. (13:4)

The great elements, the consciousness of "I," intellect and the unmanifest, the ten senses and one, and the five fields of actions of the senses, (13:5)

Desire, aversion, pleasure, pain, the whole organism, consciousness, stability–thus is the Field briefly described, and its aspects. (13:6)

Absence of pride, freedom from hypocrisy, harmlessness, fortitude, rectitude, approaching a teacher, purity, constancy and self-control, (13:7)

Detachment from the objects of sense, absence of egotism, keeping in mind the evils of birth, death, old age, disease, and pain, (13:8)

Non-attachment, absence of clinging to son, wife, home and suchlike; constant even-mindedness in desired and undesired events, (13:9)

Unswerving devotion to me with single-minded yoga, living in secluded places, having distaste for association with many people, (13:10)

Establishment in the knowledge of the Supreme Self, keeping in mind the goal of knowledge of the truth–this is said to be true knowledge. The contrary is ignorance. (13:11)

I shall explain that which must be known, knowing which

one attains immortality: the beginningless, Supreme Brahman which is said to be neither existent nor non-existent. (13:12)

With hands and feet everywhere, eyes, heads and faces everywhere, with ears throughout the universe–THAT stands, enveloping everything. (13:13)

Having the appearance of all the qualities of the senses, yet free of all the senses, unattached yet maintaining all, free from the gunas, yet experiencing the gunas, (13:14)

Outside and inside beings–the animate and the inanimate–incomprehensible because of its subtlety, far away and also near, (13:15)

Undivided, yet remaining as if divided in beings, this is to be known as the sustainer of beings, their absorber and generator. (13:16)

Also this is said to be the light of lights, beyond all darkness; knowledge, the to-be-known, the goal of knowledge seated in the heart of all. (13:17)

Thus Field, knowledge and that which must be known have been briefly stated. Comprehending all this, my devotee approaches my state of being. (13:18)

Know that both Prakriti and Purusha are beginningless; and know that the modifications and the gunas arise from Prakriti. (13:19)

Prakriti is declared to be the cause of that which is to be done, the instrument and the doer. The Purusha is declared to be the cause in the experiencing of pleasure and pain. (13:20)

The Purusha abiding in Prakriti experiences the gunas of

Prakriti; attachment to the gunas is the cause of its birth in good and evil wombs. (13:21)

The Supreme Spirit in this body is called the witness and the consenter, the supporter, the experiencer, the Great Lord, and also the Supreme Self. (13:22)

He who thus knows the Purusha and Prakriti along with the gunas, whatever be his state of evolution, he shall never be born again. (13:23)

Some perceive the Self in the Self by the Self through meditation, others by Sankhya yoga, and still others by karma yoga. (13:24)

Others, also, not knowing thus yet hearing from others, worship. They also cross beyond death, devoted to what they have heard. (13:25)

Know this: whatever is born, the animate or the inanimate, know it to be resulting from the union of the Field and the Knower of the Field. (13:26)

He who sees the Supreme Lord existing in all beings equally, not dying when they die–he sees truly. (13:27)

Truly seeing the same Lord existing everywhere, he injures not the Self by the lower self. Then he goes to the Supreme Goal. (13:28)

He who himself sees thus: that all actions are performed exclusively by Prakriti, and perceives that therefore he is himself not the doer–he sees truly. (13:29)

When he perceives the various states of being as resting in the One, and their expansion from that One alone–he then attains Brahman. (13:30)

This eternal Supreme Self, without beginning and devoid of gunas, even though dwelling in the body, does not act, nor is it tainted. (13:31)

As the all-pervading ether because of its subtlety is not tainted, so the Self seated in the body is not tainted at any time in any situation. (13:32)

As the sun alone illumines this entire world, so the Lord of the field illumines the entire field. (13:33)

Those who know through the eye of knowledge the distinction between the Field and the Knower of the Field, and the liberation of beings from Prakriti—they go to the Supreme (the Highest). (13:34)

* "In some of the books you will not find this verse. If you include this verse also, the number of verses of the Bhagavad Gita will come to 701. Some commentators look upon this verse as an interpolation" (Swami Sivananda in his Gita commentary). "This first unnumbered stanza does not occur in all versions. It may have been deleted in order to make the total number of verses an even seven hundred" (Winthrop Sargeant in his translation of the Gita).

Om Tat Sat

Thus in the Upanishads of the glorious Bhagavad Gita, the science of the Eternal, the scripture of Yoga, the dialogue between Sri Krishna and Arjuna, ends the thirteenth discourse entitled: The Yoga of the Distinction Between the Field and the Knower of the Field.

Chapter Fourteen

THE YOGA OF THE DIVISION OF THE THREE GUNAS

The Holy Lord said:
Again I shall explain to you the highest of knowledges, the best of all knowledge, having known which all the sages attained to the highest perfection. (14:1)

Resorting to this knowledge they attain identity with me. At creation they are not born, nor do they tremble at its dissolving. (14:2)

For me great Brahma is the womb, and in that do I place the seed. The origination of all beings comes from that. (14:3)

Whatever be the forms produced within all wombs, the great Brahma is their womb, and I the seed-casting Father. (14:4)

Sattwa, rajas, and tamas—these gunas born of Prakriti bind fast in the body the imperishable embodied one (the Atman-Self). (14:5)

Of these, sattwa is stainless, luminous, and health-giving; it binds by attachment to happiness and by attachment to knowledge. (14:6)

Know rajas' nature is passion arising from thirst and attachment; it binds fast the embodied one by attachment to action. (14:7)

Know indeed that tamas is born of ignorance, deluding all embodied ones. It binds by distraction, laziness and sleep. (14:8)

Sattwa causes attachment to happiness, rajas causes attachment to action; and tamas, veiling knowledge, causes attachment to delusion. (14:9)

Sattwa prevails over rajas and tamas; and rajas prevails over sattwa and tamas; and tamas prevails over sattwa and rajas. (14:10)

When the light of knowledge shines in all the gates of the body, then it should be known that sattwa is dominant. (14:11)

Greed, activity, undertaking of actions, restlessness, and desire–these arise when rajas is dominant. (14:12)

Darkness, inertia, heedlessness and delusion–these arise when tamas is dominant. (14:13)

When the embodied one dies when sattwa is dominant, then he enters the stainless realms of the knowers of the Highest. (14:14)

Dying in rajas, he is born amid those attached to action. Dying in tamas, he is born from the wombs of the deluded. (14:15)

They say the fruit of action performed well, is sattwic and without fault; but the fruit of rajas is pain, and the fruit of tamas is ignorance. (14:16)

From sattwa arises knowledge; and from rajas arises greed; from tamas arises heedlessness, delusion and ignorance. (14:17)

Those established in sattwa go upward; the rajasic remain in the middle; the tamasic, abiding in the lowest guna, go downward. (14:18)

When the beholder sees no doer other than the gunas, and knows that which is higher than the gunas, he attains to my being. (14:19)

When an embodied being rises above these three gunas, which are the source of the body, freed from birth, death, old age and pain, he attains immortality. (14:20)

Arjuna said:

By what marks is he known who has gone beyond the gunas? What is his conduct, and how does he go beyond these three gunas? (14:21)

The Holy Lord said:

He neither detests the presence nor desires the absence of illumination or activity or delusion. (14:22)

He who sits apart, indifferent to and unmoved by the gunas, realizing: "the gunas are operating," stands firm and is unwavering. (14:23)

The same in pain or in pleasure, self-contained, to whom a clod of earth, a stone, and gold are alike; to whom the liked and the unliked are the same, steadfast, to whom blame and praise of himself are equal, (14:24)

Indifferent in honor and dishonor, impartial toward the side of friend or enemy, renouncing all undertakings–he is said to be beyond the gunas. (14:25)

And he who serves me with the yoga of unswerving devotion, going beyond the three gunas, is fit for absorption in Brahman. (14:26)

For I am the abode of Brahman, the immortal, immutable, abode of everlasting dharma and of absolute bliss. (14:27)

Om Tat Sat

Thus in the Upanishads of the glorious Bhagavad Gita, the science of the Eternal, the scripture of Yoga, the dialogue between Sri Krishna and Arjuna, ends the fourteenth discourse entitled: The Yoga of the Division of the Three Gunas.

Chapter Fifteen

THE YOGA OF THE SUPREME SPIRIT

The Holy Lord said:
They speak of the eternal ashwattha tree with roots above and branches below, its leaves the Vedic hymns; he who knows it is a knower of the Vedas. (15:1)

Below, above, its branches spread afar, nourished by the gunas. Its buds are the sense-objects; and in the world of men below its roots engender action. (15:2)

Its form is not perceptible here in the world, nor its end, nor its beginning, nor its foundation. Cutting this firm-rooted ashwattha tree with the strong axe of non-attachment, (15:3)

Then that place is to be sought to which, having gone, they do not return again: "In that Primeval Purusha from which streamed forth the ancient Power, I take refuge." (15:4)

Without pride or delusion, with the evil of attachment conquered, constantly dwelling in the Self, with desires dispelled, freed from the pair of opposites known as pleasure and pain, the undeluded reach the eternal Goal. (15:5)

There the sun, moon or fire illuminate not; going whither they return not, for that is my Supreme Abode. (15:6)

Merely a fragment of myself, becoming an eternal jiva in this world of jivas, draws to itself the senses, and the mind as the sixth sense, abiding in Prakriti. (15:7)

When the Lord takes on a body, and when he leaves it, he takes the senses and the mind and goes, like the wind takes the scents from their seats, the flowers and herbs. (15:8)*

Presiding over hearing, sight, touch, taste and smell as well as the mind, this Ishwara experiences the objects of the senses. (15:9)

Whether departing, remaining or enjoying, accompanied by the gunas, the deluded do not see him. Those with the eye of knowledge see him. (15:10)

The yogis, striving, behold him dwelling within the Self; but the undeveloped and unintelligent, even though striving, see him not. (15:11)

That light which resides in the sun, which illumines the whole world, which is in the moon and in fire–know that light to be mine. (15:12)

Entering the earth, I support all beings with my energy. Having become the watery moon, I cause all plants to thrive. (15:13)

Becoming the digestive fire, I abide in the body of all living beings. Joined with prana and apana, I digest the fourfold food. (15:14)

Seated within the hearts of all, from me come memory and knowledge and their loss: I alone am to be known by all the Vedas; I am the Author of the Vedanta, and the Knower of the Vedas. (15:15)

There are two purushas in this world–the perishable and the imperishable. All beings are the perishable, and Kutastha is called the imperishable. (15:16)

But there is also the Highest Purusha, called the Supreme Self, the eternal Ishwara, Who pervades all the three worlds and sustains them. (15:17)

Since I transcend the perishable and am also above the imperishable, so in this world and in the Veda I am known as the Supreme Purusha. (15:18)

He who, undeluded, thus knows me as the Supreme Purusha, he, knowing all, worships me with his whole being. (15:19)

This most secret teaching has been imparted by me; awakened to this, a man becomes wise and all his duties are fulfilled. (15:20)

* According to the upanishads and the Gita, Ishwara lives in the heart, the core, of every human being, and experiences all which they experience. Therefore Krishna underlines that both the incarnating jivatman and the Paramatman enter and depart from the body together.

Om Tat Sat

Thus in the Upanishads of the glorious Bhagavad Gita, the science of the Eternal, the scripture of Yoga, the dialogue between Sri Krishna and Arjuna, ends the fifteenth discourse entitled: The Yoga of the Supreme Spirit.

Chapter Sixteen

THE YOGA OF THE DIVISION BETWEEN THE DIVINE AND THE DEMONIC

The Holy Lord said:

Fearlessness, purity of being, steadfastness in knowledge and yoga, almsgiving, self-control, sacrifice, self-study, tapasya, and straightforwardness, (16:1)

Non-violence, truthfulness, absence of anger, renunciation, tranquility, without calumny, compassion for beings, uncovetousness, gentleness, modesty, absence of fickleness, (16:2)

Vigor, patience, fortitude, purity, absence of hatred, absence of pride–they are the endowment of those born to a divine state. (16:3)

Hypocrisy, arrogance, conceit, anger, harshness and ignorance are the endowment of those born to a demonic state. (16:4)

The divine state is deemed to lead to liberation, the demonic to bondage. Do not grieve: you are born for a divine state. (16:5)

There are two types of beings in this world: the divine and the demonic. The divine has been described at length. Hear from me of the demonic. (16:6)

Demonic men know not what to do or refrain from; purity is not found in them, nor is good conduct, nor is truth. (16:7)

"The world," they say, "is without truth, without a basis, without God, produced by mutual union,* with lust for its cause—what else?" (16:8)

Holding this view, these lost souls, small-minded and of cruel deeds, arise as the enemies of the world, bent on its destruction. (16:9)

Attached to insatiable desires, full of hypocrisy, arrogance and intoxication, having accepted false ideas through delusion, they act with foul purposes. (16:10)

Clinging to boundless cares ending only in death, with gratification of desire as their highest aim—convinced that this is all— (16:11)

Bound by a hundred snares of hope, given over to desire and anger, they seek to gain by unjust means accumulation of wealth to gratify their desires. (16:12)

"Today this has been acquired by me. This I shall also obtain. This is mine, and this gain also shall be mine. (16:13)

"That enemy has been slain by me, and I shall slay others, too, for I am the Lord, I am the enjoyer, I am successful, powerful and happy. (16:14)

"I am wealthy and high-born," they say, "who else is equal to me? I shall sacrifice, I shall give, I shall rejoice." Thus, they are deluded by ignorance. (16:15)

Led astray by many imagined fancies, caught in a net of delusion, addicted to the gratifying of desire, they fall into a foul hell. (16:16)

Self-conceited, stubborn, filled with the intoxication of wealth, they sacrifice in name only, for show, not according to the prescribed forms. (16:17)

Clinging to egotism, power, haughtiness, desire and anger, these malignant people hate me in their own and in others' bodies. (16:18)

These malicious evildoers, cruel, most degraded of men, I hurl perpetually into only the wombs of demons here. (16:19)

Entering the demonic wombs, and deluded birth after birth, not attaining to me they fall into a progressively lower condition. (16:20)

Triple is the gate of this hell, destructive of the Self: desire, anger and greed. Therefore one should abandon these three. (16:21)

A man who is liberated from these three gates to darkness does what is best for him, and thus goes to the Highest Goal. (16:22)

He who casts aside the injunctions of the scriptures, following the impulse of desire, attains neither perfection nor happiness, nor the Supreme Goal. (16:23)

Therefore the standards of the scriptures should be your guide in determining what should be done and what should not be done. Knowing what the scriptural injunctions prescribe, you should perform action here in this world. (16:24)

* *Aparaspara* is translated "mutual union" by many translators into English, but it literally means "not one by the other," or "not by a succession." In his translation Judge has: "not governed by law," and Aurobindo: "a world of chance." It seems to me that the idea is denial of both cause and effect and the manifestation of the universe in an orderly and hierarchical manner according to exact laws. We are all familiar with the atheistic-materialistic ideas about the universe being without meaning, purpose or even order. It seems to me that Vyasa is indicating that such a view of the world without either God or cosmic order is demonic.

Om Tat Sat

Thus in the Upanishads of the glorious Bhagavad Gita, the science of the Eternal, the scripture of Yoga, the dialogue between Sri Krishna and Arjuna, ends the sixteenth discourse entitled: The Yoga of the Division between the Divine and the Demonic.

Chapter Seventeen

THE YOGA OF THE DIVISION
OF THREEFOLD FAITH

Arjuna said:

Those who cast aside the prescriptions of the scriptures, doing sacrifice with faith, what is their condition: sattwa, rajas or tamas? (17:1)

The Holy Lord said:

Threefold is the embodied ones' faith inherent within their nature: the sattwic, the rajasic and the tamasic. So hear of this. (17:2)

The faith of each one is according to his nature. A man consists of his faith–he is what his faith is. (17:3)

The sattwic worship the gods; the rajasic worship yakshas and rakshasas;* the others, the tamasic men, worship the spirits of the departed and hosts of nature spirits. (17:4)

Those who practice extreme austerities not ordained by the

scriptures, accompanied by hypocrisy and egotism along with the force of desire and passion, (17:5)

Senselessly torturing in the body the entire aggregates of the elements, and me within the body, know them to be of demonic resolves. (17:6)

The food also liked by each one is threefold, as is sacrifice, tapasya, and almsgiving. Hear the distinction of them. (17:7)

Foods increasing life, purity, strength, health, happiness, cheerfulness, flavorful, smooth, firm and substantial are liked by the sattwic. (17:8)

Foods that are pungent, sour, salty, excessively hot, harsh, astringent and burning, producing pain, grief, and disease are liked by the rajasic. (17:9)

That which is stale, tasteless, putrid, leftover to the next day,** the remnants of food eaten by others and impure, is the food the tamasic like. (17:10)

Sacrifice which is offered, observing the scriptures, by those who do not desire the fruits, concentrating the mind only on the thought: "This is to be offered;" that is sattwic. (17:11)

But sacrifice which is offered with a view for the fruit and for the purpose of ostentation, know that to be rajasic. (17:12)

Sacrifice devoid of faith, disregarding the scriptures, with no food offered,*** without mantras, without gift or fee**** is declared to be tamasic. (17:13)

Reverence for the gods, the twice-born, teachers and the wise; purity, straightforwardness, brahmacharya and non-injury: these are called tapasya of the body. (17:14)

Speech which causes no distress or vexation, truthful, pleasant, beneficial, instruction in the knowledge of the Self: these are called tapasya of speech. (17:15)

Tranquility of mind, kindliness, silence, self-control and purity of the mental state: these are called tapasya of the mind. (17:16)

This threefold tapasya practiced with the highest faith by those without desire for fruits and steadfast, is considered to be sattwic. (17:17)

Tapasya which is practiced with hypocrisy to gain acceptance, honor and reverence, is declared to be rajasic, unstable, and transitory. (17:18)

Tapasya which is practiced with deluded notions of the Self, and self-torture, or for the purpose of harming another, is declared to be tamasic. (17:19)

That gift which is given with the thought: "It is to be given," to a worthy person, one who has done no prior favor to the giver, in a proper place at a proper time: that gift is considered sattwic. (17:20)

But that gift which is given with the aim of recompense, or with regard to the giving's fruit, or is given reluctantly, is considered rajasic. (17:21)

The gift which is given at the wrong place or time, to unworthy persons, without respect or with disdain, is declared to be tamasic. (17:22)

"Om, Tat, Sat;" this is known as the triple designation of Brahman. By this were created of old the Brahmanas, Vedas, and Sacrifice. (17:23)

Therefore the acts of sacrifice, gift and tapasya prescribed by the scriptures are always begun uttering "Om" by the Brahma-vadins (those who walk the path to Brahman). (17:24)

Uttering "Tat" without interest in fruits, acts of sacrifice, tapasya and the various acts of gift are performed by the seekers of liberation. (17:25)

"Sat" is used in its meaning of Reality and Goodness; so also the word "Sat" is used in the sense of an auspicious act. (17:26)

Steadfastness in sacrifice, tapasya and gift is called "Sat." And action in connection with these is designated as "Sat." (17:27)

Whatever is sacrificed, given or done, and whatever tapasya is practiced without faith is called "Asat." It is naught here or hereafter (after death). (17:28)

* In this verse, "yakshas and rakshasas" refers to the benevolent, semidivine beings, not the negative beings of the same name.

** Since there was no refrigeration in ancient India, no food was considered fit to eat if it sat overnight.

*** The sponsors of sacrifice or worship are considered obligated to offer food of some kind (at least sweets) to all those who attend.

**** Gifts are often given to spiritual dignitaries who attend a sacrifice or worship, and a fee is always to be given to those who perform the sacrifice or worship. Not giving a sufficient fee would also be considered "without fee."

Om Tat Sat

Thus in the Upanishads of the glorious Bhagavad
Gita, the science of the Eternal, the scripture of Yoga,
the dialogue between Sri Krishna and Arjuna, ends
the seventeenth discourse entitled: The Yoga of the
Division of Threefold Faith.

Chapter Eighteen

THE YOGA OF LIBERATION BY RENUNCIATION

Arjuna said:
I desire to know separately the essential nature of sannyasa and tyaga. (18:1)

The Holy Lord said:
The renunciation of actions arising from desire the sages understand as sannyasa. The abandonment of the fruits of all action the wise declare to be tyaga. (18:2)

Some men of wisdom declare that all action should be abandoned as an evil, while others declare that sacrifice, gift and tapasya should not be abandoned. (18:3)

Hear from me the conclusion regarding tyaga. Tyaga has been designated to be of three kinds. (18:4)

Acts of sacrifice, gift and tapasya should not be abandoned, but should be done. Sacrifice, gift and tapasya are purifiers of the wise. (18:5)

However these works should indeed be performed, abandoning attachment and the fruits. Such is my highest and certain conviction. (18:6)

But renunciation of obligatory action is not proper. Abandonment of these from delusion is declared to be tamasic. (18:7)

He who abandons action from fear of trouble or of pain, does not obtain the fruit of that renunciation; he performs rajasic renunciation. (18:8)

When action is done because it is a duty (ought to be done), disciplined, having abandoned attachment and the fruit as well, that renunciation is considered sattwic. (18:9)

The man of renunciation, wise, filled with sattwa, with doubt eliminated, does not dislike disagreeable work, nor is he attached to agreeable work. (18:10)

Truly, embodied beings are not able to give up actions entirely; but he who relinquishes the fruit of action is called a man of renunciation. (18:11)

For those who have not renounced, the fruit of action is threefold when they depart this world: undesired, desired and mixed. But for the renouncers there is none whatever. (18:12)

Learn from me these five factors for the accomplishment of all actions, declared in the Sankhya: (18:13)

The body, the doer, the functions of various kinds, the various distinct activities, and the divine overseer as the fifth. (18:14)

Whatever action a man performs with his body, speech, or mind–either right or wrong–these are its five factors. (18:15)

This being so, he who sees himself as the actual doer does

not really see, because he does not have a perfect (complete) understanding. (18:16)

He whose state of mind is not egoistic, whose intellect is not tainted, even though he slays all these people, he does not slay, neither is he bound (by karmic consequences). (18:17)

Knowledge, the known and the knower are the threefold impulse to action. The instrument, the action and the doer are the threefold constituents of action. (18:18)

It is said in the doctrine of the three gunas (the Sankhya Philosophy) that knowledge, action and the doer are of three kinds: hear them also duly. (18:19)

That by which one sees the one indestructible Being in all beings, undivided in the divided (many)–know that knowledge to be sattwic. (18:20)

But that knowledge which sees in all beings different beings of various kinds, know that knowledge to be rajasic. (18:21)

But that knowledge which clings to a single effect as if it were the whole, and without reason, without basis in truth and trivial–that is declared to be tamasic. (18:22)

Action which is ordained and free from attachment, done without attraction or aversion, with no desire to obtain the fruit–that action is said to be sattwic. (18:23)

But that action done with desire for the fulfillment of desires, with self-centeredness, or furthermore is done with much effort, is considered rajasic. (18:24)

That action which is undertaken because of delusion, without regard to the consequences of loss, injury or one's own ability– that is said to be tamasic. (18:25)

A doer free from attachment, non-egoistic, endowed with steadfastness and resolution, and unaffected by success or failure, is said to be sattwic. (18:26)

A doer that is passionate, desiring to obtain action's fruits, greedy, violent-natured, impure, easily elated or dejected, is declared to be rajasic. (18:27)

An agent that is unsteady, vulgar, obstinate, false, dishonest, lazy, despondent and procrastinating, is said to be tamasic. (18:28)

Now hear the three kinds of intellect and steadfastness according to the gunas, set forth completely and severally. (18:29)

That intellect which knows the paths of work and renunciation, when to act and when not to act, what ought to be done and what ought not to be done, what is to be feared and what is not to be feared, bondage and liberation, is sattwic. (18:30)

That intellect which incorrectly understands dharma and adharma, what should be done and what should not be done, is rajasic. (18:31)

That intellect enveloped in darkness, regarding adharma as dharma, and seeing all things pervertedly (turned backward: that is, seeing all things completely opposite to their true nature or state), is tamasic. (18:32)

That firmness of intellect or purpose by which through yoga the functions of the mind, the vital force (prana) and the senses are restrained, is sattwic. (18:33)

But that firmness by which one holds to dharma, enjoyment and wealth from attachment and desire for the fruits of action, is rajasic. (18:34)

That firmness by which a stupid person does not abandon sleep, fear, depression and arrogance, is tamasic. (18:35)

Now hear from me of the threefold happiness that one enjoys through practice and by which one attains to the end of pain. (18:36)

That happiness which is like poison at first, but like amrita in the end, born of the light of one's own Self, is declared to be sattwic. (18:37)

That happiness arising from the contact of the senses with their objects, which in the beginning is like amrita but changes into that which is like poison, is declared to be rajasic. (18:38)

That happiness which in the beginning and as a result is delusive of the Self, arising from sleep, indolence and heedlessness, is declared to be tamasic. (18:39)

There is no being either on earth, nor yet in heaven among the gods, that can exist free from these three gunas born of Prakriti. (18:40)

Of the Brahmins, the Kshatriyas and the Vaishyas, as also the Shudras, the duties* are distributed according to the qualities of their swabhava. (18:41)

Tranquility, self-restraint, tapasya, purity, patience, uprightness, knowledge, realization and belief in God–these are the duties of Brahmins, born of their swabhava. (18:42)

Valor, splendor, steadfastness, skill, not fleeing in battle, generosity and lordliness of spirit are the duties of Kshatriyas, born of their swabhava. (18:43)

Agriculture, cow-herding and trade are the duties of the Vaishyas, born of their swabhava, and the Shudras' duty is doing service, born of their swabhava. (18:44)

Satisfied in his own duty, a man attains perfection. Hear how he who is happy in his own duty (swakarma) finds perfection. (18:45)

By worshipping with his swakarma him from whom all beings have their origin, by whom all this universe is pervaded, a man finds perfection. (18:46)

Better is one's own swadharma, though imperfect, than another's duty, though well performed. Performing the duty prescribed by one's own nature (swabhava) produces no fault. (18:47)

The duty to which one is born should not be abandoned, although faulty, for all undertakings are enveloped by defects as is fire by smoke. (18:48)

He whose intellect (buddhi) is unattached, whose lower self is subdued, from whom desire has departed, by renunciation attains the supreme state of freedom from action. (18:49)

Learn from me in brief how one who has attained perfection also attains Brahman, that supreme state of knowledge. (18:50)

Endowed with a supremely pure intellect, controlling the lower self by firmness, turning from the objects of the senses, beginning with sound, casting off attraction and aversion, (18:51)

Dwelling in a solitary place, eating lightly (what is easily digested), with speech, body and mind controlled, constantly devoted to yoga meditation, taking refuge in vairagya, (18:52)

Forsaking egotism, force, pride, desire, anger, possessiveness, freed from the notion of "mine" and peaceful—he is fit for union with Brahman. (18:53)

Absorbed in Brahman, with Self serene, he grieves not nor desires, the same to all beings, he attains supreme devotion unto me. (18:54)

By devotion to me he comes to know how great I am in truth, then having known me in truth, he forthwith enters into me. (18:55)

Doing all actions, always taking refuge in me, by my grace he attains the eternal, immutable state. (18:56)

Mentally renouncing all actions in me, holding me as the highest goal, resorting to buddhi-yoga, constantly fix your mind on me. (18:57)

Fixing your mind on me, you shall by my grace surmount all obstacles; but if from egotism you will not hear me, then you shall perish. (18:58)

If, filled with egotism, you think: "I will not fight," this your resolve shall be in vain, for your nature will compel you. (18:59)

What you do not wish to do, through delusion, you shall do against your will, bound by your karma born of your own nature. (18:60)

The Lord dwells in the hearts of all beings, causing them by his maya to revolve as if mounted on a machine. (18:61)

Fly unto him alone for refuge with your whole being. By that grace you shall attain supreme peace and the eternal abode. (18:62)

Thus has the knowledge that is more secret than all that is secret been expounded to you by me. Having reflected on this fully, act in the way you wish. (18:63)

Hear again my highest teaching, most secret of all, because you are dearly loved by me; therefore I shall tell you what is for your good. (18:64)

Fix your mind on me, be devoted to me, sacrifice and bow down to me. In this way you shall truly come to me, for I promise you–you are dear to me. (18:65)

Abandoning all duties, take refuge in me alone; then I shall free you from all demerits, do not grieve. (18:66)

This should not be spoken of by you at any time to one who is without tapasya, nor to one who is not dedicated, nor to one who does not desire to listen, nor to one who speaks evil of (mocks) me. (18:67)

He who with supreme devotion to me teaches this supreme secret unto my devotees shall doubtless come to me. (18:68)

And no one among all men shall do more pleasing service to me, nor shall there be another on the earth dearer to me than he. (18:69)

And he who will study this dharmic dialogue of ours, by him will I have been worshipped through the sacrifice of knowledge; such is my conviction. (18:70)

Even the man who hears this, full of faith and not scoffing, he also, liberated, shall attain the happy worlds of those of righteous deeds. (18:71)

Has this been heard by you with a one-pointed mind? Has the delusion of your ignorance been destroyed? (18:72)

Arjuna said:
My delusion is destroyed, and I have regained my knowledge

through your grace; I am firm and my doubts are gone. I will act according to your word. (18:73)

Sanjaya said:

Thus have I heard this wondrous dialogue of Krishna and the great-souled Arjuna, which causes the hair to stand on end. (18:74)

By the grace of Vyasa have I heard this supreme and most secret yoga directly from Krishna, Yoga's Lord, himself declaring it. (18:75)

O King, remembering again and again this marvelous dialogue between Krishna and Arjuna, I rejoice again and again. (18:76)

And remembering again and again that most marvelous form of Krishna, great is my wonder, O King, and I rejoice again and again. (18:77)

Wherever there is Krishna, Yoga's Lord, wherever is Arjuna the bowman, there will forever be splendor, victory, wealth and righteousness: this is my conviction. (18:78)

* In this section of verses, "duty" is the usual translation of "actions" (karma), and cannot be objected to, but in these verses it also means the actions that will be done by the different castes, impelled by their innate nature (swabhava). In other words, these are the things that will be done, and the qualities revealed, spontaneously by the various castes. Caste is not determined by action, but action is produced by the innate caste-nature, the swabhava.

Om Tat Sat

Thus in the Upanishads of the glorious Bhagavad Gita,
the science of the Eternal, the scripture of Yoga, the
dialogue between Sri Krishna and Arjuna, ends the
eighteenth discourse entitled: The Yoga of Liberation
by Renunciation.

Glossary

Abhyasa: Sustained (constant) spiritual practice.

Abhyasa Yoga: Yoga, or union with God, through sustained spiritual practice.

Adharma: Unrighteousness; demerit, failure to perform one's proper duty; unrighteous action; lawlessness; absence of virtue; all that is contrary to righteousness (dharma).

Adhibhuta: Primal Being; pertaining to the elements; the primordial form of matter.

Adhidaiva: Primal God.

Adhiyajna: Primal Sacrifice; Supreme Sacrifice.

Adhyatma: The individual Self; the supreme Self; spirit.

Adityas: Solar deities, the greatest of which is Vishnu.

Agni: Fire; Vedic god of fire.

Ahankara: Ego; egoism or self-conceit; the self-arrogating principle "I," "I" am-ness; self-consciousness.

Ahimsa: Non-injury in thought, word, and deed; non-violence; non-killing; harmlessness.

Airavata: The white elephant of Indra that was produced by the churning of the ocean.

Amrita: That which makes one immortal. The nectar of immortality that emerged from the ocean of milk when the gods churned it.

Ananta: Infinite; without end; endless; a name of Shesha, the chief of the Nagas, whose coils encircle the earth and who symbolizes eternity, and upon whom Vishnu reclines.

Anarya(n): Not aryan; ignoble; unworthy. See Aryan.

Apana: The prana that moves downward, producing the excretory functions in general; exhalation.

Aparigraha: Non-possessiveness, non-greed, non-selfishness, non-acquisitiveness; freedom from covetousness; non-receiving of gifts conducive to luxury.

Arjava(m): Straightforwardness; simplicity; honesty; rectitude of conduct (from the verb root *rinj*: "to make straight"); uprightness.

Arjuna: The great disciple of Krishna, who imparted to him the teachings found in the Bhagavad Gita. The third of the Pandava brothers who were major figures in the Mahabharata War. His name literally means "bright," "white," or "clear."

Arya(n): One who is an Arya–literally, "one who strives upward." Both Arya and Aryan are exclusively psychological terms having nothing whatsoever to do with birth, race, or nationality. In his teachings Buddha habitually referred to spiritually qualified people as "the Aryas." Although in English translations we find the expressions: "The Four Noble Truths," and "The Noble Eightfold Path," Buddha actually said: "The Four Aryan Truths," and "The Eightfold Aryan Path."

Aryaman: Chief of the Pitris.

Ashwattha: The pippal (sacred fig) tree, in the Bhagavad Gita, the eternal tree of life whose roots are in heaven. The "world tree" in the sense of the axis of the earth and even of the cosmos.

Ashwins: Two Vedic deities, celestial horsemen of the sun, always together, who herald the dawn and are skilled in healing. They avert misfortune and sickness and bring treasures.

Astikyam: Piety; belief in God.

Asura: Demon; evil being (a-sura: without the light).

Asuric: Of demonic character.

Bhagavan: The Lord; the One endowed with the six attributes, viz. infinite treasures, strength, glory, splendor knowledge, and renunciation; the Personal God.

Bhrigu: An ancient sage, so illustrious that he mediated quarrels among the gods.

Bhuta: A spirit. Some bhutas are subhuman nature spirits or "elementals", but some are earthbound human spirits–ghosts. Bhutas may be either positive or negative.

Brahma: The Creator (Prajapati) of the three worlds of men, angels, and archangels (Bhur, Bhuwah, and Swah); the first of the created beings; Hiranyagarbha or cosmic intelligence.

Brahmachari(n): One who observes continence; a celibate student in the first stage of life (ashrama); a junior monk.

Brahmacharya: Continence; self-restraint on all levels; discipline; dwelling in Brahman.

Brahman: The Absolute Reality; the Truth proclaimed in the Upanishads; the Supreme Reality that is one and indivisible, infinite, and eternal; all-pervading, changeless Existence; Existence-knowledge-bliss Absolute (Satchidananda); Absolute Consciousness; it is not only all-powerful but all-power itself; not only all-knowing and blissful but all-knowledge and all-bliss itself.

Brahmana: A Vedic liturgical text explaining the rituals found in the Vedic samhitas (collection of hymns). A guidebook for performing those rites.

Brahmanirvana: The state of liberation (nirvana) that results from total union with Brahman.

Brahmavada: The Path to Brahman; the way to supreme enlightenment.

Brahmavadin: Literally "one who walks the path of Brahman." One who advocates that there is one existence alone–Parabrahman.

Brahmin (Brahmana): A knower of Brahman; a member of the highest Hindu caste consisting of priests, pandits, philosophers, and religious leaders.

Brihaspati: The guru–priest and teacher–of the gods.

Brihatsaman: A hymn to Indra found in the Sama Veda.

Buddhi: Intellect; intelligence; understanding; reason; the thinking mind; the higher mind, which is the seat of wisdom; the discriminating faculty.

Buddhi Yoga: The Yoga of Intelligence spoken of in the Bhagavad Gita which later came to be called Jnana Yoga, the Yoga of Knowledge.

Car-warrior: See Maharatha.

Caste: See Varna.

Chandra: Presiding deity of the moon or the astral lunar world (loka).

Chitraratha: The chief of the gandharvas.

Daityas: Demons who constantly war with the gods. Sometimes "races" or nationalities who acted contrary to dharma and fought against the "aryas" were also called demons (daityas or asuras); giant; titan..

Deva: "A shining one," a god–greater or lesser in the evolutionary hierarchy; a semi-divine or celestial being with great powers, and therefore a "god." Sometimes called a demi-god. Devas are the demigods presiding over various powers of material and psychic nature. In many instances "devas" refer to the powers of the senses or the sense organs themselves.

Dharma: The righteous way of living, as enjoined by the sacred scriptures and the spiritually illumined; characteristics; law; lawfulness; virtue; righteousness; norm.

Dharmic: Having to do with dharma; of the character of dharma.

Dhrita: Steadfastness; constancy; sustained effort; firmness; patience; endurance.

Dukha(m): Pain; suffering; misery; sorrow; grief; unhappiness; stress; that which is unsatisfactory.

Dwesha: Aversion/avoidance for something, implying a dislike for it. This can be emotional (instinctual) or intellectual. It may range from simple non-preference to intense repulsion, antipathy and even hatred. See Raga.

Dwija: "Twice born;" any member of the three upper castes that has received the sacred thread (yajnopavita).

Gandharva: A demigod–a celestial musician and singer.

Ganga: See Ganges.

Ganges (Ganga): The sacred river–believed to be of divine origin–that flows from high up in the Himalayas, through the plains of Northern India, and empties into the Bay of Bengal. Hindus consider that bathing in the Ganges profoundly purifies both body and mind.

Garuda: A great being who can assume bird form, and therefore considered the king of birds. Often depicted as an eagle, he is the vehicle of Vishnu.

Gayatri Meter: A meter found only in the Rig Veda, consisting of three lines of eight syllables each. It is considered especially appropriate for mantric invocation of deities before worship.

Ghee: Clarified butter.

Guna: Quality, attribute, or characteristic arising from nature (Prakriti) itself; a mode of energy behavior. As a rule, when "guna" is used it is in reference to the three qualities of Prakriti, the three modes of energy behavior that are the basic qualities of nature, and which determine the inherent characteristics of all created things. They are: 1) sattwa–purity, light, harmony; 2) rajas–activity, passion; and 3) tamas–dullness, inertia, and ignorance.

Guru: Teacher; preceptor; spiritual teacher or acharya.

Indra: King of the lesser "gods" (demigods); the ruler of heaven (Surendra Loka); the rain-god.

Ishwara: "God" or "Lord" in the sense of the Supreme Power, Ruler, Master, or Controller of the cosmos. "Ishwara" implies the powers of omnipotence, omnipresence, and omniscience.

Janaka: The royal sage (raja rishi) who was the king of Mithila and a liberated yogi, a highly sought-after teacher of philosophy in ancient India. Sita, the wife of Rama, was his adopted daughter.

Jiva: Individual spirit.

Kalpa: A Day of Brahma–4,320,000,000 years. It alternates with a Night of Brahma of the same length. He lives hundred such years. Brahma's life is known as Para, being of a longer duration than the life of any other being, and a half of it is called Parardha. He has now completed the first Parardha and is in the first day of the second Parardha. This day or Kalpa is known as Svetavarahakalpa. In the Day of Brahma creation is manifest and in the Night of Brahma is it resolved into its causal state.

Kamadeva: God of beauty and love; the Vedic Cupid who shoots a bow with flowers instead of arrows.

Kamadhenu: Wish-fulfilling cow produced at the churning of the milk ocean.

Kamadhuk: See Kamadhenu.

Kandarpa: See Kamadeva.

Kapila: The great sage who formulated the Sankhya philosophy which is endorsed by Krishna in the Bhagavad Gita. (See the entry under Sankhya.)

Karma: Karma, derived from the Sanskrit root *kri*, which means to act, do, or make, means any kind of action, including thought and feeling. It also means the effects of action. Karma is both action and reaction, the metaphysical equivalent of the principle: "For every action there is an equal and opposite reaction." "Whatsoever a man soweth, that shall he also reap" (Galatians 6:7). It is karma operating through the law of cause and effect that binds the jiva or the individual soul to the wheel of birth and death. There are three forms of karma: sanchita, agami, and prarabdha. Sanchita karma is the vast store of accumulated actions done in the past, the fruits of which have not yet been reaped. Agami karma is the action that will be done by the individual in the future. Prarabdha karma is the action that has begun to fructify, the fruit of which is being reaped in this life.

Karma Yoga: The Yoga of selfless (unattached) action; performance of one's own duty; service of humanity.

Karma Yogi: One who practices karma yoga.

Karmakanda: The ritual portion of the Veda. The philosophy that Vedic ritual is the only path to perfection.

Kshatriya: A member of the ruler/warrior caste.

Kubera: The god of wealth.

Kusha: One of the varieties of sacred grass (darbha) used in many religious rites. Because of its insulating qualities, both physical and metaphysical, it is recommended as a seat (asana) for meditation, and as mats for sleeping (it keeps the sleeper warm).

Kutastha: Immutable; absolutely changeless; not subject to change; literally: "summit abiding" or "on the summit." He who is found without exception in all creatures from Brahma or the creator down to ants and Who is shining as the Self and dwells as witness to the intellect of all creatures; rock-seated; unchanging; another name for Brahman.

Mahapralaya: The final cosmic dissolution; the dissolution of all the worlds of relativity (Bhuloka, Bhuvaloka, Swaloka, Mahaloka, Janaloka, Tapaloka, and Satyaloka), until nothing but the Absolute remains. There are lesser dissolutions, known simply as pralayas, when only the first five worlds (lokas) are dissolved.

Maharatha: "A great-car-warrior," a commander of eleven thousand bowmen as he rode in his chariot.

Manava: Man; a human being; a descendant of Manu.

Manava dharma: The essential nature of man; religion of man; the duties of man.

Manu: The ancient lawgiver, whose code, The Laws of Manu (Manu Smriti) is the foundation of Hindu religious and social conduct.

Manus: Progenitors of the human race who were also its lawgivers and teachers.

Margashirsha: A lunar month, roughly the latter half of November and the first half of December. This is the time of ideal weather in India.

Marichi: The chief of the Maruts.

Maruts: The presiding deities of winds and storms.

Maya: The illusive power of Brahman; the veiling and the projecting power of the universe, the power of Cosmic Illusion. "The Measurer"–a reference to the two delusive "measures," Time and Space.

Meru: The mountain, of supreme height, on which the gods dwell, or the mountain on which Shiva is ever seated in meditation, said to be the center of the world, supporting heaven itself–obviously a yogic symbol of the spinal column or merudanda. The name of the central bead on a japa mala (rosary).

Moha: Delusion–in relation to something, usually producing delusive attachment or infatuation based on a completely false perception and evaluation of the object.

Naga: Snake; naked; a kind of powerful spirit-being worshipped in some areas of India, possessing great psychic powers and the ability to appear and communicate with human beings; one order of Sadhus, who are nude.

Narada: A primeval sage to whom some of the verses of the Rig Veda are attributed.

Om: The Pranava or the sacred syllable symbolizing and embodying Brahman. See the book *Om Yoga Meditation*.

Pandavas: The five sons of King Pandu: Yudhishthira, Bhima, Arjuna, Nakula, and Sahadeva. Their lives are described in the Mahabharata.

Pandus: See Pandavas.

Papa(m): Sin; demerit; evil; sinful deeds; evil deeds.

Parigraha: Possessiveness, greed, selfishness, acquisitiveness; covetousness; receiving of gifts conducive to luxury.

Pavaka: Agni.

Pitamaha: Grandfather; Great Father; titles of Brahma, the Creator.

Pitri: A departed ancestor, a forefather.

Prahlada: A daitya prince who rejected his daitya heritage and became a devotee of Vishnu. His father, the evil Hiranyakashipu, tortured him and attempted his life because of his devotion and his speaking to others of divine matters, yet he remained steadfast.

Prajapati: Progenitor; the Creator; a title of Brahma the Creator.

Prakriti: Causal matter; the fundamental power (shakti) of God from which the entire cosmos is formed; the root base of all elements; undifferentiated matter; the material cause of the world. Also known as Pradhana. Prakriti can also mean the entire range of vibratory existence (energy).

Pralaya: Dissolution. See Mahapralaya.

Prana: Life; vital energy; life-breath; life-force; inhalation. In the human body the prana is divided into five forms: 1) Prana, the prana that moves upward; 2) Apana: The prana that moves downward, producing the excretory functions in general. 3) Vyana: The prana that holds prana and apana together and produces circulation in the body. 4) Samana: The prana that carries the grosser material of food to the apana and brings the subtler material to each limb; the general force of digestion. 5) Udana: The prana which brings up or carries down what has been drunk or eaten; the general force of assimilation.

Preta: Ghost; spirit of the dead.

Purusha: "Person" in the sense of a conscious spirit. Both God and the individual spirits are purushas, but God is the Adi (Original, Archetypal) Purusha, Parama (Highest) Purusha, and the Purushottama (Highest or Best of the Purushas).

Purushottama: The Supreme Person; Supreme Purusha; the Lord of the universe. (See Purusha.)

Raga: Blind love; attraction; attachment that binds the soul to the universe. Attachment/affinity for something, implying a desire for it. This can be emotional (instinctual) or intellectual. It may range from simple liking or preference to intense desire and attraction. Greed; passion. See Dwesha.

Rajas: Activity, passion, desire for an object or goal.

Rajasic: Possessed of the qualities of the raja guna (rajas).

Passionate; active; restless.

Rajoguna: Activity, passion, desire for an object or goal.

Rakshasa: There are two kinds of rakshasas: 1) semidivine, benevolent beings, or 2) cannibal demons or goblins, enemies of the gods. Meat-eating human beings are sometimes classed as rakshasas.

Rama: An incarnation of God–the king of ancient Ayodhya in north-central India. His life is recorded in the ancient epic Ramayana.

Rishi: Sage; seer of the Truth.

Rudras: "Roarers;" Vedic deities of destruction for renewal, the chief of which is Shiva; storm gods.

Sadhyas: A group of celestial beings with exquisitely refined natures thought to inhabit the ether.

Sama Veda: A collection of Rig Veda hymns that are marked (pointed) for singing. It is sometimes spoken of as the "essence" of the Rig Veda.

Samsara: Life through repeated births and deaths; the wheel of birth and death; the process of earthly life.

Sankalpa: A life-changing wish, desire, volition, resolution, will, determination, or intention–not a mere momentary aspiration, but an empowering act of will that persists until the intention is fully realized. It is an act of spiritual, divine creative will inherent in each person as a power of the Atma.

Sankhya: One of the six orthodox systems of Hindu philosophy whose originator was the sage Kapila, Sankhya is the original Vedic philosophy, endorsed by Krishna in the Bhagavad Gita (Gita 2:39; 3:3,5; 18:13,19), the second chapter of which is entitled "Sankhya Yoga." *A Ramakrishna-Vedanta Wordbook* says: "Sankhya postulates two ultimate realities, Purusha and Prakriti. Declaring that the cause of suffering is man's identification of Purusha with Prakriti and its products, Sankhya teaches that liberation and true knowledge are attained in the supreme consciousness, where such identification ceases and Purusha is realized as existing independently in its transcendental nature." Not surprisingly, then, Yoga is based on the Sankhya philosophy.

Sannyas(a): Renunciation; monastic life. Sannyasa literally means "total [san] throwing away [as]," absolute rejection.

Sannyasi(n): A renunciate; a monk.

Sapta Rishis: "Seven Sages." Great Beings who exist at the top of creation and supervise it.

Sarva(m): All; everything; complete.

Sattwa: Light; purity; harmony, goodness, reality.

Sattwa Guna: Quality of light, purity, harmony, and goodness.

Sattwic: Partaking of the quality of Sattwa.

Shankara: "The Auspicious One." A title of Shiva.

Shudra: A member of the laborer, servant caste.

Siddha: A perfected–liberated–being, an adept, a seer, a perfect yogi.

Skanda: Subramanya; the god of war and son of Shiva and Parvati; Skanda.

Soma: A milkweed, *Ascelpias acida*, whose juice in Vedic times was made into a beverage and offered in sacrifices; the nectar of immorality; a name of Chandra, the presiding deity of the moon.

Sudarshana Chakra: The invincible weapon of Lord Vishnu which is able to cut through anything, and is a symbol of the Lord's power of cutting through all things which bind the jiva to samsara. Thus it is the divine power of liberation (moksha).

Swabhava: One's own inherent disposition, nature, or potentiality; inherent state of mind; state of inner being.

Swadharma: One's own natural (innate) duty (dharma, based on their karma and samskara. One's own prescribed duty in life according to the eternal law (ritam).

Swakarma: Action, duty, business or occupation determined by (according to) one's own innate nature.

Tamas: Dullness, darkness, inertia, folly, and ignorance.

Tamasic: Possessed of the qualities of the tamo guna (tamas). Ignorant; dull; inert; and dark.

Tapasya: Austerity; practical (i.e., result-producing) spiritual discipline; spiritual force. Literally it means the generation of heat or energy, but is always used in a symbolic manner, referring to spiritual practice and its effect, especially the roasting of karmic seeds, the burning up of karma.

Tyaga: Literally: "abandonment." Renunciation–in the Gita, the relinquishment of the fruit of action.

Tyagi: A renouncer, an ascetic.

Uchchaishravas: The name of Indra's horse (or the horse of the Sun god, Surya), that was born of the amrita that was churned from the ocean by the gods. The name means "high-sounding" and refers to the power of mantra.

Uchchishta[m]: The remnants of food eaten by others, the actual leavings from someone's plate, considered extremely unclean physically and psychically. (This does not apply to food left in a serving dish or cooking vessel unless someone ate from it rather than serving it on their own dish.)

Ushanas: An ancient seer and poet.

Ushmapas: A class of ancestors (pitris) which live off subtle emanations or vapors.

Vairagya: Non-attachment; detachment; dispassion; absence of desire; disinterest; or indifference. Indifference towards and disgust for all worldly things and enjoyments.

Vaishya: A member of the merchant, farmer, artisan, businessman caste.

Varna: Caste. (Literally: color.) In traditional Hindu society there were four divisions or castes according to the individual's nature and aptitude: Brahmin, Kshatriya, Vaishya, and Shudra.

Varuna: A Vedic deity considered the sustainer of the universe and also the presiding deity of the oceans and water. Often identified with the conscience.

Vasava: A name of Indra.

Vasudeva: "He who dwells in all things"–the Universal God; the father of Krishna, who is himself also sometimes called Vasudeva.

Vasuki: The king of the serpents. He assisted at the churning of the milk ocean.

Vasus: Eight Vedic deities characterized by radiance.

Vayu: The Vedic god of the wind; air; vital breath; Prana.

Vedas: The oldest scriptures of India, considered the oldest scriptures of the world, that were revealed in meditation to the Vedic Rishis (seers). Although in modern times there are said to be four Vedas (Rig, Sama, Yajur, and Atharva), in the upanishads only three are listed (Rig, Sama, and Yajur). In actuality, there is only one Veda: the Rig Veda. The Sama Veda is only a collection of Rig Veda hymns that are marked (pointed) for singing. The Yajur Veda is a small book giving directions on just one form of Vedic sacrifice. The Atharva Veda is only a collection of theurgical mantras to be recited for the cure of various afflictions or to be recited over the herbs to be taken as medicine for those afflictions.

Vedic: Having to do with the Vedas.

Vijnana: The highest knowledge, beyond mere theoretical knowledge (jnana); transcendental knowledge or knowing; experiential knowledge; a high state of spiritual realization–intimate knowledge of God in which all is seen as manifestations of Brahman; knowledge of the Self.

Vishnu: "The all-pervading;" God as the Preserver.

Vishuddha: Supremely pure; totally pure.

Vishwa devas: A group of twelve minor Vedic deities.

Vrishnis: The clan to which Krishna belonged.

Vyasa: One of the greatest sages of India, commentator on the Yoga Sutras, author of the Mahabharata (which includes the Bhagavad Gita), the Brahma Sutras, and the codifier of the Vedas.

Yadava: "Descendant of Yadu" an ancient Indian king; the Yadavas, a clan of India, were descended from King Yadu; a title of Krishna, since he was part of the Yadava clan. Swami

Bhaktivedanta, founder of the Hare Krishna movement in the West, as well as some anthropologists, believed that the Yadava clan, who disappeared from India shortly after Krishna's lifetime, emigrated to the middle east and became the people we know today as the Jews, Abraham having been a Yadava.

Yajna: Sacrifice; offering; sacrificial ceremony; a ritual sacrifice; usually the fire sacrifice known as agnihotra or havan.

Yaksha: There are two kinds of yakshas: 1) semidivine beings whose king is Kubera, the lord of wealth, or 2) a kind of ghost, goblin, or demon.

Yama: Yamaraja; the Lord of Death, controller of who dies and what happens to them after death.

Yoga: Literally, "joining" or "union" from the Sanskrit root yuj. Union with the Supreme Being, or any practice that makes for such union. Meditation that unites the individual spirit with God, the Supreme Spirit. The name of the philosophy expounded by the sage Patanjali, teaching the process of union of the individual with the Universal Soul.

Yogamaya: The power of Maya, of divine illusion. It is Maya in operation, the operation/movement rising from the presence (union–yoga) of God (Ishwara) within it, and therefore possessing delusive power.

Yogeshwara: Lord of Yoga; a name of Lord Krishna.

Yogi(n): One who practices Yoga; one who strives earnestly for union with God; an aspirant going through any course of spiritual discipline.

Yuga: Age or cycle; aeon; world era. Hindus believe that there are four yugas: the Golden Age (Satya or Krita Yuga), the Silver age (Treta Yuga), The Bronze Age (Dwapara Yuga), and the Iron Age (Kali Yuga). Satya Yuga is four times as long as the Kali Yuga; Treta Yuga is three times as long; and Dwapara Yuga is twice as long. In the Satya Yuga the majority of humans use the total potential–four-fourths–of their minds; in the Treta Yuga, three-fourths; in the Dwapara Yuga, one half; and in the Kali Yuga, one fourth. (In each Yuga there are those who are using either more or less of their minds than the general populace.) The Yugas move in a perpetual circle: Ascending Kali Yuga, ascending Dwapara Yuga, ascending Treta Yuga, ascending Satya Yuga, descending Satya Yuga, descending, Treta Yuga, descending Dwapara Yuga, and descending Kali Yuga–over and over. Furthermore, there are yuga cycles within yuga cycles. For example, there are yuga cycles that affect the entire cosmos, and smaller yuga cycles within those greater cycles that affect a solar system. The cosmic yuga cycle takes 8,640,000,000 years, whereas the solar yuga cycle only takes 24,000 years. At the present time our solar system is in the ascending Dwapara Yuga, but the cosmos is in the descending Kali Yuga. Consequently, the more the general mind of humanity develops, the more folly and evil it becomes able to accomplish.

Did you enjoy reading this book?

Thank you for taking the time to read *The Bhagavad Gita— The Song of God*. If you enjoyed it, please consider telling your friends or posting a short review at Amazon.com, Goodreads, or the site of your choice.

Word of mouth is an author's best friend and much appreciated.

ABOUT THE AUTHOR

Abbot George Burke (Swami Nirmalananda Giri) is the founder and
director of the Light of the Spirit
Monastery (Atma Jyoti Ashram) in
Cedar Crest, New Mexico, USA.

In his many pilgrimages to India,
he had the opportunity of meeting
some of India's greatest spiritual figures,
including Swami Sivananda of Rishi-
kesh and Anandamayi Ma. During his
first trip to India he was made a member of the ancient Swami
Order by Swami Vidyananda Giri, a direct disciple of Param-
hansa Yogananda, who had himself been given sannyas by the
Shankaracharya of Puri, Jagadguru Bharati Krishna Tirtha.

In the United States he also encountered various Christian
saints, including Saint John Maximovich of San Francisco and
Saint Philaret Voznesensky of New York. He was ordained
in the Liberal Catholic Church (International) to the priest-
hood on January 25, 1974, and consecrated a bishop on
August 23, 1975.

For many years Abbot George has researched the identity of Jesus Christ and his teachings with India and Sanatana Dharma, including Yoga. It is his conclusion that Jesus lived in India for most of his life, and was a yogi and Sanatana Dharma missionary to the West. After his resurrection he returned to India and lived the rest of his life in the Himalayas.

He has written extensively on these and other topics, many of which are posted at OCOY.org.

LIGHT OF THE SPIRIT
MONASTERY

Light of the Spirit Monastery is an esoteric Christian monastic community for those men who seek direct experience of the Spirit through meditation, sacramental worship, discipline and dedicated communal life, emphasizing the inner reality of "Christ in you the hope of glory," as taught by the illumined mystics of East and West.

The public outreach of the monastery is through its website, OCOY.org (Original Christianity and Original Yoga). There you will find many articles on Original Christianity and Original Yoga, including *Esoteric Christian Beliefs*. *Foundations of Yoga* and *How to Be a Yogi* are practical guides for anyone seriously interested in living the Yoga Life.

You will also discover many other articles on leading an effective spiritual life, including *The Yoga of the Sacraments* and *Spiritual Benefits of a Vegetarian Diet*, as well as the "Dharma for Awakening" series–in-depth commentaries on these spiritual classics: the Upanishads, the Bhagavad Gita, the Tao Teh King and the Aquarian Gospel of Jesus the Christ.

Recently added are a series of podcasts by Abbot George on meditation, the Yoga Life, and remarkable spiritual people he has met in India and elsewhere, at http://ocoy.org/podcasts/

Get your FREE Meditation Guide

Sign up for the Light of the Spirit Newsletter and get *Ten Simple Tips to Improve Your Meditation Today.*

Get free updates: newsletters, blog posts, and podcasts, plus exclusive content from Light of the Spirit Monastery.

Visit: http://ocoy.org/newsletter-registration

READING FOR AWAKENING

Light of the Spirit Press presents books on spiritual wisdom and Original Christianity and Original Yoga. From our "Dharma for Awakening" series (practical commentaries on the world's scriptures) to books on how to meditate and live a successful spiritual life, you will find books that are informative, helpful, and even entertaining.

Light of the Spirit Press is the publishing house of Light of the Spirit Monastery (Atma Jyoti Ashram) in Cedar Crest, New Mexico, USA. Our books feature the writings of the founder and director of the monastery, Abbot George Burke (Swami Nirmalananda Giri) which are also found on the monastery's website, OCOY.org.

We invite you to explore our publications in the following pages.

Find out more about our publications at
lightofthespiritpress.com

The Christ of India

The Story of Saint Thomas Christianity

There is a strong connection between Jesus and India, both historically and philosophically. And his disciple, Saint Thomas, who was the apostle of India, built upon the foundation of that connection. The result is that unique form of Christianity known as Saint Thomas Christianity.

In *The Christ of India*, Abbot George Burke presents the growing evidence that Jesus spent much of his "Lost Years" in India and Tibet, and reveals the philosophical unity of Jesus' teachings with the Eternal Way of Truth known in India as Sanatana Dharma. Also includes the history of Saint Thomas Christianity from the times of Jesus and Saint Thomas to the present day

What Readers say:

"Abbot George is like the Emily Dickinson of modern day spiritual writers."–*Reverend Gerry Nangle*

"Interpreting the teachings of Jesus from the perspective of Santana Dharma, The Christ of India is a knowledgeable yet engaging collection of authentic details and evident manuscripts about the Essene roots of Jesus and his 'Lost years'. ...delightful to read and a work of substance, vividly written and rich in historical analysis, this is an excellent work written by a masterful teacher and a storyteller." –*Enas Reviews*

Om Yoga Meditation: Its Theory and Practice

A thorough guide providing all the information that might be desired for a successful meditation practice, illumining the art and science of effective inner life. Beginning with an in-depth explanation of what yoga is and what its goals are, and continuing with a background on the theory of mantra, Abbot George then shows the value of the unique mantra Om. He shows that Om Meditation is the original yoga, citing the classic scriptures of India and the testimony of the saints.

In *Om Yoga Meditation* you will discover the techniques for using Om in meditation, and how to make your meditation the most effective. You will also learn the foundations of the yogic life that will support and nourish your practice, and be given the keys to bless others as well as yourself using Om.

What Readers say:

"*Om Yoga Meditation* uniquely touches on the spiritual power and lasting positive effects of the mantra Om. If you're curious about trying the mantra Om in your spiritual practice, this book is the perfect guide with theory and techniques to help you along the way."—*Spirituality & Health Magazine*

The Dhammapada for Awakening
A Commentary on Buddha's Practical Wisdom

The Dhammapada for Awakening brings a refreshing and timely perspective to ancient wisdom and shows seekers of inner peace practical ways to improve their inner lives today.

It explores the Buddha's answers to the urgent questions, such as "How can I find find lasting peace, happiness and fulfillment that seems so elusive?" and "What can I do to avoid many of the miseries big and small that afflict all of us?".

Drawing on the proven wisdom of different ancient traditions, and the contemporary masters of spiritual life, as well as his own studies and first-hand knowledge of the mystical traditions of East and West, Abbot George illumines the practical wisdom of Buddha in the Dhammapada, and more importantly, and make that makes that teaching relevant to present day spiritual seekers.

What Readers say:

"In this compelling book, Abbot George Burke brings his considerable knowledge and background in Christian teachings and the Vedic tradition of India to convey a practical understanding of the teachings of the Buddha. ...This is a book you'll want to take your time to read and keep as reference to reread. Highly recommended for earnest spiritual aspirants"*–Anna Hourihan, author, editor, and publisher at Vedanta Shores Press*

May a Christian Believe in Reincarnation?

Discover the real and surprising history of reincarnation and Christianity.

A growing number of people are open to the subject of past lives, and the belief in rebirth–reincarnation, metempsychosis, or transmigration–is becoming commonplace. It often thought that belief in reincarnation and Christianity are incompatible. But is this really true? May a Christian believe in reincarnation? The answer may surprise you.

Reincarnation-also known as the transmigration of souls-is not just some exotic idea of non-Christian mysticism. Nor is it an exclusively Hindu-Buddhist teaching.

In orthodox Jewish and early Christian writings, as well as the Holy Scriptures, we find reincarnation as a fully developed belief, although today it is commonly ignored. But from the beginning it has been an integral part of Orthodox Judaism, and therefore as Orthodox Jews, Jesus and his Apostles would have believed in rebirth.

What Readers say:

"Those needing evidence that a belief in reincarnation is in accordance with teachings of the Christ need look no further: Plainly laid out and explained in an intelligent manner from one who has spent his life on a Christ-like path of renunciation and prayer/meditation."
—*Christopher T. Cook*

A Brief Sanskrit Glossary

A Spiritual Student's Guide to Essential Sanskrit Terms

This Sanskrit glossary contains full translations and explanations of many of the most commonly used spiritual Sanskrit terms, and will help students of the Bhagavad Gita, the Upanishads, the Yoga Sutras of Patanjali, and other Indian scriptures and philosophical works to expand their vocabularies to include the Sanskrit terms contained in them, and gain a fuller understanding in their studies.

What Readers say:

"If you are reading the writings of Swami Sivananda you will find a basketful of untranslated Sanskrit words which often have no explanation, as he assumes his readers have a background in Hindu philosophy. For writings like his, this book is invaluable, as it lists frequently used Sanskrit terms used in writings on yoga and Hindu philosophical thought.

"As the title says, this is a spiritual students' guidebook, listing not only commonly used spiritual terms, but also giving brief information about spiritual teachers and writers, both modern and ancient.

"Abbot George's collection is just long enough to give the meanings of useful terms without overwhelming the reader with an overabundance of extraneous words. This is a book that the spiritual student will use frequently."—*Simeon Davis*

The Gospel of Thomas for Awakening

A Commentary on Jesus' Sayings as Recorded by the Apostle Thomas

"From the very beginning there were two Christianities." So begins this remarkable work. While the rest of the Apostles dispersed to various areas of the Mediterranean world, the apostle Thomas travelled to India, where growing evidence shows that Jesus spent his "Lost Years," and which had been the source of the wisdom which he had brought to the "West."

In *The Gospel of Thomas for Awakening*, Abbot George shines the "Light of the East" on the sometimes enigmatic sayings of Jesus recorded by his apostle Saint Thomas, revealing their unique and rich practical nature for modern day seekers for spiritual life.

Ideal for daily study or group discussion.

What Readers say:

"An extraordinary work of theological commentary, *The Gospel of Thomas for Awakening* is as informed and informative as it is inspired and inspiring".—*James A. Cox, Editor-in-Chief, Midwest Book Review*

Robe of Light
An Esoteric Christian Cosmology

In *Robe of Light* Abbot George Burke explores the whys and wherefores of the mystery of creation. From the emanation of the worlds from the very Being of God, to the evolution of the souls to their ultimate destiny as perfected Sons of God, the ideal progression of creation is described. Since the rebellion of Lucifer and the fall of Adam and Eve from Paradise flawed the normal plan of evolution, a restoration was necessary. How this came about is the prime subject of this insightful study.

Moreover, what this means to aspirants for spiritual perfection is expounded, with a compelling knowledge of the scriptures and of the mystical traditions of East and West.

What Readers say:

"Having previously read several offerings from the pen of Abbot George Burke I was anticipating this work to be well written and an enjoyable read. However, Robe of Light actually exceeded my expectations. Abbot Burke explicates the subject perfectly, making a difficult and complex subject like Christian cosmology accessible to those of us who are not great theologians."—*Russ Thomas*

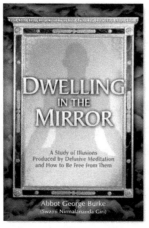

Dwelling in the Mirror

A Study of Illusions Produced by Delusive Meditation and How to Be Free from Them

"There are those who can have an experience and realize that it really cannot be real, but a vagary of their mind. Some may not understand that on their own, but can be shown by others the truth about it. For them and those that may one day be in danger of meditation-produced delusions I have written this brief study." –*Abbot George Burke*

In *Dwelling in the Mirror* you will learn:

• different types of meditation and the experiences they produce, and the problems and delusions which can arise from them.
• how to get rid of negative initiation energies and mantras.
• what are authentic, positive meditation practices and their effects and aspects.
• an ancient, universal method of meditation which is both proven and effective.

What Readers say:

"I totally loved this book! After running across many spiritual and self-help books filled with unrealistic promises, this little jewel had the impact of a triple Espresso."

—Sandra Carrington-Smith, author of *Housekeeping for the Soul*

Spiritual Benefits of a Vegetarian Diet

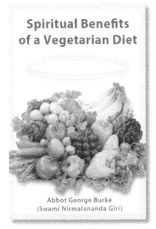

Spiritual Benefits of a Vegetarian Diet

Abbot George Burke
(Swami Nirmalananda Giri)

The health benefits of a vegetarian diet are well known, as are the ethical aspects. But the spiritual advantages should be studied by anyone involved in meditation, yoga, or any type of spiritual practice.

Although diet is commonly considered a matter of physical health alone, since the Hermetic principle "as above, so below" is a fundamental truth of the cosmos, diet is a crucial aspect of emotional, intellectual, and spiritual development as well. For diet and consciousness are interrelated, and purity of diet is an effective aid to purity and clarity of consciousness.

The major thing to keep in mind when considering the subject of vegetarianism is its relevancy in relation to our explorations of consciousness. We need only ask: Does it facilitate my spiritual growth–the development and expansion of my consciousness? The answer is Yes.

A second essay, *Christian Vegetarianism,* continues with a consideration of the esoteric side of diet, the vegetarian roots of early Christianity, and an insightful exploration of vegetarianism in the Old and New Testaments.

Available as a free Kindle ebook download at Amazon.com.

Foundations of Yoga

Ten Important Principles Every Meditator Should Know

An in-depth examination of the important foundation principles of Patanjali's Yoga, Yama & Niyama.

Yama and Niyama are often called the Ten Commandments of Yoga, but they have nothing to do with the ideas of sin and virtue or good and evil as dictated by some cosmic potentate. Rather they are determined on a thoroughly practical, pragmatic basis: that which strengthens and facilitates our yoga practice should be observed and that which weakens or hinders it should be avoided.

It is not a matter of being good or bad, but of being wise or foolish. Each one of these Five Don'ts (Yama) and Five Do's (Niyama) is a supporting, liberating foundation of Yoga. An introduction to the important foundation principles of Patanjali's Yoga: Yama & Niyama

Available as a free Kindle ebook download at Amazon.com.

Notes